PRAISE FOR JAMES RESTON, JR.

The Conviction of Richard Nixon

"A compact and gripping behind-the-scenes narrative...intelligent, passionate."
— Matthew Dallek, *Washington Post Book World*

" Reston has crafted a riveting memoir... a welcome flashback for those still infatuated with one of America's darkest political hours."
—*Los Angeles Times*

"[*The Conviction of Richard Nixon*] plunges us right into the unholy mind of the most disgraced president...in US history."
— *Salon.com*

"Political history that reads like a thriller. Passionate, intelligent, entertaining, and human."
—Michael Sheen costar of *Frost/Nixon*

Warriors of God

"Splendid and thrilling... a wonderfully told story."
— *The New York Times Book Review*

"James Reston Jr. ...devotes his gift for words to the construction of a thrilling narrative."
—*The Economist*

"A refreshingly unbiased popular history of the Third Crusade."
— *The Washington Post Book World*

"Reading this book, one sways between horror and exhilaration. The magnitude of human suffering is mind boggling, but the warriors' adventures are the stuff of boyhood fantasy."

– *Forbes*

"Remarkably intimate and engagingly detailed."

- *Kirkus Reviews*

FRAGILE INNOCENCE

"A page turning read... Reston has turned the writer's lens on his own family to tell this intensely personal story. Most of all, though, it's the story of a father's discovery- the discovery that love trumps terror, that love finds expression despite seemingly impossible circumstances. It is, in the end, the story of a father's love for his daughter."

- *Washington Post Book World*

"A moving memoir."   *–People*

"Candid...a story of love and hope."   *–Newsweek*

DEFENDERS OF THE FAITH

" A readable, enjoyable and professional popular history of a crucial era of Muslim-Christian conflict... The obvious relevance of this book is the twenty-first-century challenge to the West of radical Islam. [The book has] fascinating echoes with modern conflicts and strategic dilemmas."

– *The Washington Times*

"Reston helps the lay reader grasp the root causes of religious tensions that exist to this day between Protestant and Catholic, Christian and Muslim, and Sunni and Shiite. Fast-paced and engaging, this is excellent reading."

—Library Journal

Dogs of God

"Engaging and highly readable…The events in *Dogs of God* may have taken place more than 500 years ago, but there are times when they seem chillingly, worryingly familiar."

—The Washington Post Book World

"Colorful and readable…Reston paint a vivid picture of a myriad of Christian, Jewish and Muslim characters playing out the dramas of fifteenth century Spain."

— Jerusalem Post

"A vividly told narrative history."   *—The Guardian*

"A highly entertaining, thoughtful and complex narrative that both introduces and analyzes a greatly misunderstood era."

—Publisher's Weekly

"Energetic…Reston brings alive the conflict between Catholic and Muslim and how the outcome still resonates today."

—USA Today

ALSO BY JAMES RESTON, JR.

To Defend, To Destroy: A Novel, 1971

The Amnesty of John David Herndon, 1973

The Knock at Midnight, a novel, 1975

The Innocence of Joan Little: A Southern Mystery, 1977

Our Father Who Art in Hell: The Life and Death of the Reverend Jim Jones, 1981

Sherman's March and Vietnam, 1985

Lone Star: The Life of John Connally, 1989

Collision at Home Plate: The Lives of Pete Rose and Bart Giamatti, 1991

Galileo: A Life, 1994

The Last Apocalypse: Europe at the Year 1000 A.D., 1999

Warriors of God: Richard the Lionheart and Saladin in the Third Crusade, 2001

Dogs of God: Columbus, the Inquisition, and the Defeat of the Moors, 2005

Fragile Innocence: A Father's Memoir of His Daughter's Courageous Journey, 2006

The Conviction of Richard Nixon: The Untold Story of the Frost/Nixon Interviews, 2007

Defenders of the Faith: Charles V, Suleyman the Magnificent, and the Battle for Europe, 1520–1536, 2009

THE ACCIDENTAL VICTIM
JFK, Lee Harvey Oswald, and the Real Target in Dallas

By James Reston, Jr.

Exclusive History Book Club Edition
published by

ASSEMBLY!
PRESS

All the images in the book are Warren Commission exhibits and therefore, public domain except the following
1. George de Mohrenschildt: Corbis
2. JFK speaking in the rain at Fort Worth: Sen. Yarborough, Connally, and LBJ in the background; **credit line**: Art Rickerby/Time & Life Picture/Getty Images
3. Breakfast in Fort Worth, Jackie seated, JFK on right, LBJ on left: **credit line**: Art Rickerby/Time & Life Picture/Getty Images
4. "Dallas Loves you." Book cover photo and in text: **credit line**: Library of Congress
5. Connally leaving Parkland Hospital in wheelchair: **credit line**: AP Photo/Ted Powers
6. Connally and Nellie Connally at eternal flame, 1964: **credit line**: AP Photo
7. Senator Yarborough weeping: **credit line**: Library of Congress
8. Credit for the author picture: Christopher Casler
9. Credit for front cover limo picture: Library of Congress

Cover design by Lauren Panepinto
Interior design by Amanda McPherson

Exclusive History Book Club Edition published by Zola Books and Assembly! Press.

Zola Books
242 W 38th St, 2nd Floor
New York, NY 10018
www.zolabooks.com

Assembly! Press
An Imprint of Bookspan
250 West 34th Street
New York, NY 10019

The Zola Books name and logo are trademarks of Zola Books.

The Assembly! Press name and logo are trademarks of Bookspan.

The publisher is not responsible for websites (or their content) that are not owned by the publisher.

First print edition: September 2013

ISBN: 978-1-62490-870-5

000 001

CONTENTS

For Stewart Udall

PREFACE

The fiftieth anniversary of the Dallas assassination of President John F. Kennedy is sure to be marked with great and solemn attention, as it deserves to be. One needs only to look at the pictures of the presidential motorcade on November 22, 1963, as it passed through the narrow streets of downtown Dallas and see the spectators reach out and nearly touch the president in his open convertible, to wonder at how the world has changed. The terrible event is one of those times, like most recently the events of 9/11, during which anyone who was alive and conscious remembers with great vividness. Back then I was a 22-year-old research assistant (and later speech writer) for Kennedy's Secretary of the Interior, Stewart Udall. Udall was gone that day, flying to Japan on a trade mission with other Cabinet members. When the news came, the staff huddled around the television in the secretary's back room, listening to Walter Cronkite deliver the news, in utter disbelief and horror.

Over these five decades, a warehouse of books and articles and films has been created about the murder and the Commission that investigated it. One would think that "history" had come to a definite consensus. How far from the case that is! Was there one assassin or several? Was a foreign government behind the deed, or some gangster group? It has even been suggested that Lyndon Johnson, Kennedy's successor, was somehow involved, or the CIA or the FBI. The theories and conjectures abound. And the farther we get from the event, the more truth seems to elude us. In a recent poll of Americans, 85% expressed belief in a conspiracy, even though no convincing evidence has been put forward to support that notion.

This book is profoundly, unabashedly anti-conspiracy. The evidence is overwhelming that Lee Harvey Oswald acted alone, with absolutely no encouragement from, or involvement with, a foreign government or a criminal organization. But the matter does not end there. Why would this wretched man with a ninth-grade education and a demonstrable admiration for President Kennedy pick up a rifle and set out on such a dastardly mission that day?

I could never accept the explanation of the august Warren Commission: that Oswald was possessed by grandiose notions and, as a convinced Marxist, hoped to bring down the U.S. government by decapitating its head. There had to be something deeply emotional in his makeup and visceral in his instincts that engaged his anger, an anger so great that it became a murderous rage.

This book sets out to find that source. It substantially elaborates on my argument about the assassination that began with a *Time* magazine cover story marking the twenty-fifth anniversary of Dallas, November 28, 1988, and continued with my treatment of the event in my biography of John Connally, *The Lone Star*, published the following year. In addition, I further develop my argument, first put forward in a 11/22/05 *Los Angeles Times* op-ed piece, that focuses on the critical role played by JFK's back brace in those five critical seconds along Elm Street in Dealey Plaza. In the winter of 2013, accompanied by Dr. Lawrence Altman, the distinguished medical reporter for the *New York Times* and my colleague at the Woodrow Wilson International Center for Scholars, I viewed that corset at the National Archives in College Park, MD, as the first writer ever to do so.

Sometimes attacking a great and significant historical event from an oblique angle can lead to astonishing surprises. That was my experience here.

CHAPTER ONE:

The Assassin

L ee H. Oswald, as he signed his letters, was a small, wiry
loner, twenty-four years of age. He considered Fort
Worth to be his home, and he had left it with a splash
that had made front-page headlines in the *Star Telegram* every
bit as large as those used a year later when President Kennedy
appointed Fort Worth oilman John Connally to be Secretary
of the Navy:

FORT WORTH MAN TO BECOME A RED
AND WRITE A BOOK?
FORT WORTH DEFECTOR CONFIRMS
RED BELIEFS
MY VALUES DIFFERENT, DEFECTOR
TOLD MOTHER
TURNCOAT HANGS UP ON MOTHER

The details were lurid and shocking. Oswald had dropped

out of high school after his freshman year to join the Marine Corps. His three-year hitch in the corps began with an average qualification as a sharpshooter, proceeded through electronics and radar training, and had concluded with a tour in Atsugi, Japan, on a base from which U-2 aircraft took off for Russia.

Then, reported the Fort Worth paper, the "turncoat" had read *Das Kapital* as he defended freedom in Japan. In his last months in the service, he had thought of nothing but defection and had saved all his money ($1,600) to travel to the Soviet Union. Later, while he languished in the sumptuous Metropole Hotel in Moscow awaiting final word on his citizenship application, he submitted to an interview by UPI. Why did he want to defect? He gave three reasons: racial discrimination, the treatment of the underdog, and the hate in his native land.

Lee Harvey Oswald's façade was abrasive and petulant, but his adventure in Russia began with the pathos of Dostoevski-an tale. He had taken a ship from New Orleans to Great Britain, and then had flown to Helsinki, a point from which he believed the entry into Russia would somehow be easier. Arriving at Soviet soil early in October, he brashly approached his Intourist agent, a stolid woman named Rimma, and blurted out that he wished to apply for Soviet citizenship. In the days that followed, the sympathetic Rimma took him through the necessary gates, helping him with his letter to the Supreme Soviet and, on his twentieth birthday – October 18, 1959 – sweetly presenting him with a copy of Dostoevsky's *The Idiot*. Three days later, however, Oswald's colossal effort of will was imperiled. In his diary he described his response (the spelling errors are Oswald's):

October 12: Meeting with single official. Balding, stout, black suit, fairly good English, askes what do I want. I say Soviet citizenship. He tells me 'USSR only great in literature and wants me to go back home.' I am stunned. I reiterate. He says he shall check and let me know whether my visa will be extended. (It exipiers foday.)

Eve. 6.00 Recive word from police official. I must leave country tonight at 8 P.M. as visa expirs. I am shocked!! My dreams! I retire to my room. I have $100 left. I have waited for 2 year to be accepted. My fondes dreams are shattered because of a petty offial, because of bad planning, I planned to much! 7.00P.M. I decided to end it. Soak rist in cold water to numb the pain Than slash my left wrist. Than plaung wrist into bath tub of hot water. I think when Rimma comes at 8 to find me dead, it will be a great shock. Somewhere a violin plays, as I watch my life whirl away. I think to myself. 'how easy to die' and 'a sweet death' (to violins) about 8.00. Rimma finds my unconscious (bathtub water a rich. red color) She screams (I remember that…Poor Rimma stays by my side as interrpator far into the night. I tell her to go home (my mood is bad) but she stays. She is my friend. She has a strong will. Only at this moment, I notice she is preety.

Upon his release from the hospital a week later, Oswald again confronted the daunting face of Soviet bureaucracy, but this time the strange American was taken more seriously. His passport did not seem to be enough for them, so Oswald presented his most prized possession, a laminated card that displayed his honorable discharge from the Marine

Corps. Throughout all that transpired after his discharge, Oswald defined himself through his Marine Corps service. The corps had shaped him. It proved his importance. He flaunted it now with the hope that the Soviets would see how big a catch he was. Delay the inevitable. Three days later, as he clattered around his hotel room at the Metropole, he was tormented with anxiety and loneliness, writing:

Oct 30: I have been in hotel three days. It seems like three years. I must have some sort of showdown!

The next day he slipped out of the hotel and took a cab to the American embassy. There he presented himself to a wry and experienced professional named Richard Snyder. Snyder found him to be a well-dressed, intelligent, and very determined twenty-year-old. Oswald got right to the point. Slapping his passport down on the desk, he demanded the right to renounce his American citizenship. By no means was Snyder unprepared for the situation. Some weeks earlier, Snyder had processed a renunciation of American citizenship for another American named Petrulli. He too had applied for Soviet citizenship. But the Soviets had decided that they did not want Petrulli, who turned out to be a mental case, and Snyder had to do a good deal of fudging to reassert American authority and annul the renunciation. With Oswald, he was determined to stall as long as he could, although he knew he could not do so forever. Oswald was fully within his rights. If Oswald was in command of his senses, which he certainly appeared to be, the action was, Snyder cautioned him, permanent and irrevocable.

Snyder tried to draw Oswald out, asking him a number of soft questions and stressing the enormous import of what the

Oswald at time of his renunciation

young man proposed to do. At one point, Snyder asked him his reasons.

"I am a Marxist!" Oswald replied histrionically, as if that covered all the bases.

"Well, then," replied the affable Mr. Snyder, "you're going to be very lonesome in the Soviet Union." Oswald was not amused.

Aggressive and strident, Oswald would not be deterred. Finally, Snyder seized upon the bureaucrat's final pretext: the embassy was technically closed that afternoon for the weekend. The applicant would have to come back in a few days. Oswald stormed out.

Instead of returning the following business week, Oswald wrote the embassy an outraged letter, charging that the consul had denied him his legal right to renounce and that his application for citizenship was now pending before the Supreme Soviet. In a final flourish, which the American consul later recalled to be distinctly "Oswaldish" in its comical pomposity and sonorousness, Oswald wrote,

"In the event [the acceptance of my application to the Supreme Soviet], I shall request my government to lodge a formal protest regarding this incident."

In his interview with Snyder, Oswald had made one threat that could not be ignored. He promised to turn over to the Soviets all the military secrets he had learned in the Marines. As a radar operator with a secret clearance, he had access to all tactical call signs, the relative strength of squadrons, the number and type of aircraft in each, the names of commanding officers, and the authentication code for entering and exiting the Air Defense Identification Zone, as well as radio frequencies and the range of radar both for his squadron and squadrons contiguous to his own.

Immediately, Snyder alerted the naval attaché in the embassy, who wired the Navy Department in Washington. As a result, codes, aircraft call signs, and radio and radar frequencies in the scope of Oswald's knowledge were changed. Certain things, however, could not be changed, such as the frequency range of the new height-finding radar, just introduced at enormous cost into the Marine Corps air defense system. In its displeasure, the Navy Department initiated action against Oswald which would, four years later, devastate him and for which he would come to blame John Connally.

As he moped around the Metropole Hotel, Oswald's sole link to America and to his past was his older brother, Rob-

Oswald letter, Nov. 1959, renouncing US citizenship

ert. Robert Oswald had reached Lee by telegram in early November, calling his decision to defect a mistake. On November 26, Lee replied angrily in a long letter, full of cant:

"See the segregation. See the unemployment and what au-
tomation is. Remember how you were laid off at Convair. I
will ask you a question, Robert: what do you support the
American government for? What is the ideal you put forward? Do not say 'freedom' because freedom is a word used
by all peoples through all of time. Ask me, and I will tell you
I fight for *communism.*"

Toward the end of his harangue, he declared the importance of ideology over blood. He had four parting shots: "1.
In the event of war I would kill *any* American who put on a
uniform in defense of the American government, any American. 2. In my own mind, I have no attachments of any kind
to the U.S. 3. I want to – and I shall – live a normal, happy,
and peaceful life here in the Soviet Union *for the rest of my
life.* 4. My mother and you are *not* objects of affection, but
only examples of workers in the U.S. You should not try to
remember me in any way I used to be... I am not all bitterness
or hate. I come here only to find freedom."

"In truth," he said in closing, "I feel I am at last with my
own people."

After this flourish, Oswald receded into the proletariat. If
he expected to be fussed over, to be made a hero in the Soviet state, he was disappointed. The KGB took no interest
in him. He was never questioned about his military service
in Japan, nor about new American radars or about U-2 aircraft. He was considered "not very bright" and the local au-

Oswald and fellow workers in radio-TV factory, Minsk

thorities in Minsk, where he was sent to work in a radio factory, were requested to keep an eye on him, lest he turn out to be some sort of "sleeper agent."

Nevertheless, for the first nine months of his expatriation, Oswald's dream for a "normal, happy, and peaceful life" in Russia was a reality. He found the work in the factory easy. His fellow workers treated him warmly, especially as he began to acquire the language. If he was not accorded a hero's status, he was, nevertheless, given special treatment. Assigned an apartment with a splendid view overlooking the Svislach River, he raked in 1,400 rubles a month, twice the salary of other workers on his level. Seven hundred rubles was a supplement from a mysterious branch of the Red Cross "to help out," and Oswald would crow in his diary that this income was the equivalent to that of the director of the radio factory.

"It is a Russian's dream," he wrote blissfully in March.

The summer brought rapturous walks in the deep pine forests of Byelorussia. He had joined a hunting club at the factory, and with a shotgun on his shoulder (since private ownership of rifles and pistols was forbidden in the Soviet Union) he ventured into the rural regions around Minsk. These trips made a deep impression. The peasants he met and in whose homes he sometimes stayed overnight were frequently close to starvation. Often, out of sympathy, he would leave what game he had shot. He was also fascinated by the radio speakers in the peasants' huts, that kept up a constant patter of exhortation day and night, and could not be turned off. At this early stage, however, he merely took note of these exotic aspects of the totalitarian state. Other images cut deeper.

In the fall, he rhapsodized about the golds and reds of the landscape. "Plums, peaches, apricots and cherries abound in the last fall weeks," he wrote in his diary. "I am a healthy, brown color and stuffed with fresh fruit."

With the approach of his first Russian winter, Oswald, like the hero of *The Idiot*, developed a melancholy and then a dread of the coldness and the darkness. He began to take more notice of the trappings of the Communist state around him: "I am increasingly aware of the presence of Lebizen, the shop party secretary, fat, fortyish, and jovial on the outside. He is a no-nonsense party regular."

He began to resent compulsory attendance at boring factory meetings, where the factory doors were locked, and no one ever voted 'no' to a formal proposal. He was horrified at the poor quality and the cost of simple necessities like clothes and shoes. While the slogans and exhortations of the state cluttered his mind, the dreary routine of the worker's life began to undercut his operatic dream.

The turning point for Oswald was not political, but emotional. In early January, he fell hopelessly in love with a comrade at the factory named Ella, who, after a dalliance, spurned him. In his diary, he declared that he was "misarable," and a few weeks later he wrote:

"I am starting to reconsider my desire about staying. The work is drab. The money I get has no where to be spent. No nightclubs or bowling alleys. No place of recreation acept the trade dances. I have had enough."

On February 1, he wrote to the American counsel, Richard Snyder, that he wanted to go home.

Oswald's overture at this point was exploratory. Ambivalence rather than total disaffection marked his psychology, and he was moving toward negative perceptions of both political systems.

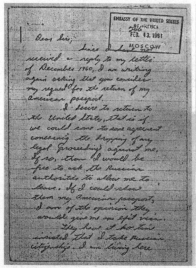 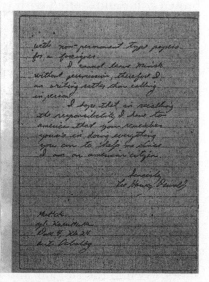

Change of heart: Oswald wants to return to US

His life took another turn in March when, at a "boring" trade union dance, he met a stubborn blonde pharmacist with a French hairdo named Marina, who had lived the first six years of her life near the Arctic Circle in Murmansk and Archangel. In contrast to Ella, who had snickered at the awkwardness of his marriage proposal, Marina encouraged his attentions. In April the two were married. In his diary he declared: "In spite of fact I married Marina to hurt Ella, I found myself in love with Marina." (This line above all others would wound Marina when the diary was published several months after Oswald's death.)

Marriage did not change his desire to get out of the Soviet Union, however. In July 1961, the Oswalds applied for an exit visa, hoping to return to America. The change in Oswald's attitude toward his adopted state was evident in a letter he wrote to Robert just after he returned from a talk with Snyder about going home:

"The Russians can be crule and very crude at times. They gave a cross examination to my wife on the first day we came from Moscow. They knew everything, because they spy and read the mails. But we shall continue to try and get out. We shall not retreat. As for your package, we never received it. I suppose they swiped that to, the bastards."

Now that Oswald had asked to go home, the cruelty of the Russians took another form. His "Red Cross" allotment of 700 rubles a month abruptly stopped. Oswald finally saw it for what it was: he had been a paid stooge. He had never told anyone of his supplement. Only when he was on his way home to Texas was he able to write about it, and even then, only to himself. The important thing is the lesson he drew from it:

*Whene I frist went to Russia in the winter of 1959 my funds were very limited. So after a certain time, after the Russians had assured thereselfs that I was really a naive american who believed in communism, they arranged for me to recive a certain amount of money every month. OK it came technically through the Red Cross as finical help to a Roos polical immigrate but it was arranged by the M.V.D. (*The Russian secret police) *I told myself it was simply because I was hungry and there was several inches of snow on the ground in Moscow at that time, but it really was payment for my denudation of the U.S. in Moscow and a clear promise that for as long as I lived in the USSR life would be very good. I didn't realize all this, of course for almost two years.*

As soon as I became completely disgusted with the Sovit Union and started negotiations with the American Embassy in Moscow for my return to the U.S. my "Red Cross" allotment was cut off.

I have never mentioned the fact of these monthly payments to anyone. I do so in order to stat that I shall never sell myself intentionally or unintentionally to anyone again.

Soon enough, the American government displayed an equivalent cruelty toward him. Lee Harvey Oswald had achieved one significant thing in his life. He had joined the U.S. Marine Corps. Despite the dislike of his mates and two courts-martial (for possessing an illegal weapon and for fighting), and despite loudly proclaiming himself to be a Marxist and gaining the barracks nickname "Oswaldskovich," he made it through. His reward after three years was an honorable discharge. In his billfold he carried the laminated proof

His Honorable Discharge card

of his achievement as if it were an executive gold card. It was a credential he would need, and need desperately, when he returned to America.

In January 1962, Oswald was attempting to control his excitement over the imminent birth of his first child and the prospect of returning to the United States. On January 5 he wrote to Robert.

"I really do not trust these people, so I shall wait until I'm in the U.S. before I become overjoyed."

Two weeks later the blow struck. He received a letter from his mother, Marguerite, informing him that the Marine Corps had, summarily and without a proper hearing, changed his discharge from honorable to dishonorable. The downgrading had actually stopped at "undesirable," one notch short of "dishonorable," but that was bad enough. Anything less than an honorable military discharge is a curse in America, especially for the working man, and Oswald knew it instinctively. The news was fresh only to Lee Harvey Oswald. The action had been taken a year and a half earlier.

For two years his mother had not known where her son was, or even if he was still alive, but she had labored bravely with letters to the departments of Defense and State, to House Speaker Sam Rayburn from Bonham, Texas and Congressman Jim Wright from Fort Worth, to overturn the Marine Corps decision or at least to obtain a fair hearing. In her anguish, during her son's long silence, Marguerite Oswald had seized upon the comforting notion that her son had been hypnotized and drugged by the Russians before he was carted off to the evil empire.

To Mrs. Oswald, Lee's name had been "dishonored" more by the Marine Corps actions than by her son's apparent defection. In one letter to the navy, she said she hoped the corps "would do something about this awful thing of a dishonorable discharge, because I have grandchildren....My whole family has served in the service, and Lee served the service for three years. I want his name cleared."

Lee Harvey Oswald was devastated at the news. That he would care at all is noteworthy. Why should a true convert to Communism, one so desperate for political action, one so ready to take up arms against America – in short, a person who was described by the Warren Commission as a Marxist – have even a moment of anxiety over what the fascist United States and its most dangerous military force might do in his buried military records? The true believer would be amused. But Oswald did care. He cared deeply. At bottom, his military service gave meaning to his life – beyond his new family it was the *only* thing that did.

Immediately, he sat down to write letters of complaint about the injustice. He had a valid case. His discharge had been changed for actions he took not in the Marine Corps but as a private citizen afterwards. It had been changed without a fair hearing, upon the basis of rumors that were largely unsubstantiated and upon statements like his threat to turn over military secrets that were made at a moment of high stress, and which, in fact, he never carried out. Perhaps more important than the emotional impact were the practical consequences. As he prepared to go home, Oswald knew intuitively that his road to America would be far rougher now.

On January 30, 1961, his campaign began with a letter to the Secretary of the Navy, since the Navy Department held sway over the U.S. Marine Corps. That secretary was John Connally.

From the beginning of his public life in politics, during his brief, year-long stint as Secretary of the Navy at the beginning of the Kennedy Administration, through his victorious 1962 campaign and his ascension to the governorship in January 1963 and with his first bold speeches as the state's chief executive, John Connally epitomized the big man of Texas. In his elegant books he stood with the wealthy over the poor, the business executive over the working man, white over black and Hispanic, the glamorous over the commonplace. In short, he symbolized Texas royalty over Texas peasantry. He was a taunting, polarizing figure, engendering feelings of intense

loyalty and utter contempt, even hate. His first term as governor began in a decisive year of change in America, when
political passions were overheated, though they had not yet
reached the boiling point, and where hate mail and threats
on lives were common. America was in the throes of racial
revolution.

That was all in the future. In January 1961 Connally had
only just assumed his sub-cabinet post and was little-known
in Washington except as a protégé of the new Vice President,
Lyndon Johnson. In a long-forgotten speech Connally had
nominated Lyndon Johnson for president at the Democratic
Convention of 1956.

In his schoolboy scrawl, full of his usual misspellings and
awkward constructions, now made more awkward by the syn-
tax of the Russian language, Oswald pleaded his case grandly. He began with a reference to the common bond he shared
with Secretary Connally, calling the secretary's attention to a
case "about which you may have personal knowledge since you
are a resident of Fort Worth as am I." The Fort Worth papers,
he wrote Connally, had blown his case into "another turncoat
sensation" when, in fact, he had come to Russia to reside "for
a short time, much in the same way E. Hemingway resided in
Paris."

"I have and always had the full sanction of the U.S. Embassy, Moscow, USSR," he lied, and now that he was returning to
the United States, "I shall employ all means to right this gross
mistake or injustice to a boni-fied U.S. citizen and ex-serviceman." He asked Connally personally to "repair the damage
done to me and my family."

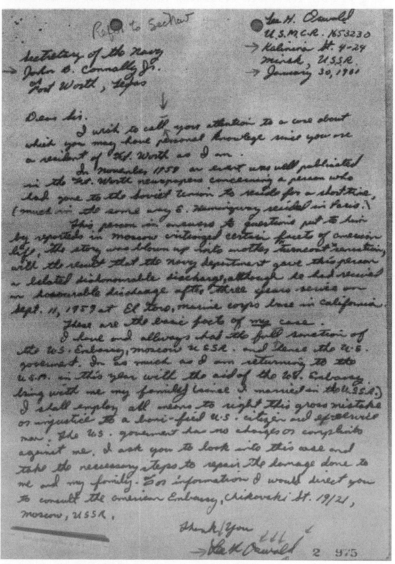

His appeal to John Connally, Secretary of Navy, Jan. 30, 1961

On the same day he wrote to Robert, who was also then living in Fort Worth, for he feared that his letter to Connally would not make it through the Russian censors. He asked Robert to be in touch with Connally independently to see how his injustice might be rectified.

Oswald did not get an answer to his plaintive letter to Connally for thirteen months. In December 1961, Connally had resigned as Secretary of the Navy and had returned to Texas to run for governor. As Oswald languished in Minsk, frustrated at the hassles he was having with the American Embassy in Moscow about his return to the States, what the ex-serviceman got from the ex-Navy Secretary on February 23, 1962 was a classic bureaucratic brush-off: a perfunctory promise to pass the problem on to his successor. Connally's letter to Oswald arrived in Minsk in a provocative, inflammatory package: a campaign envelope, with *John Connally for Governor* emblazoned on the front, and Connally's smiling face centered within a Texas star.

Thus, at the beginning of this painful journey home, Os-

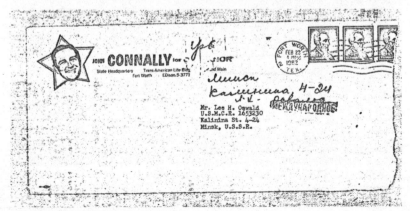

How Connally's brush-off came to Oswald

wald had been spurned by a fellow Texan, and he resented it deeply. The change in his discharge was only one, but perhaps the worst indignity that Oswald felt he had suffered. Now he had a face, in the middle of a star with a derisive smile, to go with his torment. Connally's face became the face of the U.S. government, and Connally's perfunctory snub fortified Oswald's bitterness against the country.

A cascade of slights by the naval and Marine Corps functionaries followed Connally's brush-off. A letter from the Department of Navy told Oswald that the department did not contemplate a change in the downgraded discharge. On March 22, 1962 Oswald appealed for further review. The department replied that it had no authority on the matter and sent yet another form, referring Oswald to the Navy Discharge Review Board. Oswald filled out the form in Minsk, but he did not mail it until he landed in America.

This last appeal carried the tone of moral outrage: "You have no legal or even moral right to reverse my honorable discharge." It too led nowhere. It was a classic case of a powerless nonentity mired in an endless, hopeless battle with an aloof, faceless military establishment. He would not get an official answer to his appeal for thirteen months, only four months before the assassination.

Finally, in late May 1962, the Oswalds got out of Russia.

They made their way to Rotterdam, where on June 4 they boarded the *Maasdam*, a Holland America Line ship, bound for New York. En route Oswald fell into a reflective mood, and on sheets of Holland America Line stationary, he wrote his thoughts:

Lee and Marina leaving Russia for US / Marina Oswald at train station

I wonder what would happen if somebody was to stand up and say he was utterly opposed not only to government, but to the people. too the entire land and the complete foundations of his socically [society].

Too a person knowing both systems and their factional accessories. Their can be no mediation between the systems as they exist today That person must be opposed to their basic foundations and representatives, and yet, it is immature to take the attitude which say 'a curse on both of your houses.'

In history, there are many such examples of the members of the new order rooted in the idealistical traditional of the old. As history had shown time again, the state remains and grows, whereas true democracy can be practiced only at the local level. While the centralized state, administrative, political, and or supervisual remains, their can be no real democracy, only a loose confederation of communities at a national level without any centralized state what so ever. The mass of survivors, however, will not belong too any of these groups. They will not be fanatical enough to join extremest groups and will not be too disillusioned too support either the communists of capitalist parties in their respective countriesm after the atomic catorahf [catastrophe]. They shall seek an alternative to those systems which have brought true mysery... They would deem it neccary to oppose the old systems but support at the same time their cherishe trations.

I intend to put forward just such an allturnative.

CHAPTER TWO:

Repatriation

The Oswalds arrived in Fort Worth only a few weeks before John Connally won an intense and highly publicized Democratic primary for the gubernatorial nomination. They had no money and almost no possessions, but they did have a six-month-old baby. Oswald had virtually no qualifications for employment. Worse than that, the Fort Worth paper had reported the return of the turncoat. Marina spoke no English, and her husband was determined to keep it that way.

Their isolation and hopelessness might have been even more miserable but for the help of the White Russian émigré community in the Dallas-Fort Worth area. Tightly knit and supportive, this enclave comprised about fifty people who had gravitated to Texas, most of them after the Second World War. Generally, they were already expatriates, having arrived in America from such places as Iran and Turkey, where they had fled from Russia. As a rule, they were fervently anticommunist, just as they were possessed by an enduring fascination for what was going on in Communist Russia.

The community had a titular leader, a kind and energetic gentleman in his late fifties named George Bouhe, who had fled Russia across a river into Finland in 1923. Bouhe took an immediate interest in the Oswalds and helped them to get settled by providing them with a little cash here and there, ten or twenty dollars, bringing them groceries, and helping Marina find a dentist and a pediatrician. For his pains, he got only insults from Oswald, for Oswald was determined never to accept Bouhe's kind of charity. Bouhe persisted nonetheless, mainly out of concern for Marina, who seemed to him to be a "lost soul."

To Bouhe, Oswald himself was a simpleton and a boor and, soon enough, a proven wife abuser. Moreover, from the comparative speed and ease with which the Oswalds had exited Russia, Bouhe suspected Oswald of a continuing clandestine relationship with the Soviet state. Still, he persevered because, as a matter of belief, he felt that Communism breeds among the down and out, and he hoped that a greater degree of comfort might assuage Lee Oswald's bitterness.

Bouhe's charity manifested itself in helping Oswald find work, and here Oswald ran immediately into the problem of his tainted military discharge. He was competing for the lowest rank of employment among the unskilled.

"When he went to the Texas Employment Commission in Fort Worth to ask for a job, they said what can you do?" Bouhe later told the Warren Commission. "Where did you work last? Minsk. He couldn't progress. He couldn't get anyplace." Inevitably, it came back to the discharge, since he could fudge his last place of work. "When he was applying for a job, we picked up some application blanks someplace, and you have to say about your military service. And where it says 'Discharged,' I'd ask how? And he would say, 'Put down *honorable.*'"

"That was the extent of your discussion?" the Warren Commission counsel asked.

"Right. He would freeze up like a clam."

Even though it was easy enough for any prospective employer to check his discharge claim, lying about his Marine record worked initially. Oswald's first job, acquired a month after his arrival, was at a Fort Worth welding company as a sheet-metal worker. On his application, he cited sheet-metal work in the Marine Corps as a qualification.

Bouhe confined his role with Oswald to that of an informal social worker. To discuss politics with such an ingrate was less than pointless, and Bouhe avoided the subject studiously. But the old White Russian had noticed Oswald's fixation with his military discharge. He saw how lying about it propelled Oswald into a state of high anxiety. After the assassination, after he read of John Connally's bureaucratic slight, and knowing that Oswald was especially tormented by the bad discharge at the very time when Connally was about to be promoted to the pinnacle of Texas government, Bouhe put the pieces together:

"If anybody asked me, did Oswald have any hostility towards anybody in government, I would say Governor Connally."

In early October 1962, a month before Election Day, Oswald quit his job. Apparently, he hated the hard, hot dirtiness of welding. The company was sorry to see him go. "I imagine if he had pursued that trade, he might have come out to be a pretty good sheet-metal man," his supervisor told the Warren Commission.

Precisely as this event took place, Marina and the baby took up residence in the home of Alexandra de Mohrenschildt. She was the daughter of another Russian émigré in Dallas named George de Mohrenschildt. A pompous, flamboyant dandy, de Mohrenschildt would develop an unhealthy relationship with Oswald in the months between October 1962 and March 1963. He had been born in Byelorussia in 1911, where his father had been a "marshal of nobility" in Czarist Russia before the Communists exiled him to Siberia. But the patriarch escaped to Poland, and that was where his son, George, grew up, eventually serving for a short time in the Polish army. In 1938 George emigrated to the United States. During the Second World War, the FBI took an interest in him as a possible Nazi spy, but discovered no hard evidence. A geologist by training and an executive in the oil trade, he moved smoothly in the high social circles of

George de Mohrenschildt

oil-rich Dallas. He would claim to have been friendly with Jackie Kennedy's mother, Mrs. Hugh Auchincloss, in his earlier days. In 1960 de Mohrenschildt had lost a son to cystic fibrosis, and he would later claim to the Warren Commission that his interest in Oswald as a lost boy came from his own loss of a son.

De Mohrenschildt was drawn to Oswald largely for reasons of self-amusement. To the White Russian, Oswald was a bauble, especially fun to play with when he was confused by de Mohrenschildt's brilliant arguments or awed by the émigré's elegant worldliness. In 1978 the House Assassinations Committee discovered a manuscript de Mohrenschildt was writing to work out his metaphysical responsibility. In it the émigré spoke of Oswald's admiration for Kennedy and his hatred for John Connally. The extent of Oswald's dissatisfaction with the president is contained in his reaction to the lame jokes that de Mohrenschildt would tell him.

Had Lee heard the one about what Kennedy said to the businessman? "The economic situation is so good that if I weren't your president, I would invest in the stock market right now," says the president. "So would we, if you weren't our president," replied the businessman. Oswald laughed heartily. Even better, he liked the one de Mohrenschildt told about Kennedy's terrible nightmare: the president sits bolt upright one night in bed, turns to his wife, and says, "Jackie, honey, I just dreamt that I was spending my own money and not the government's." Oswald laughed heartily at that as well, "but without resentment," de Mohrenschildt reported.

"Lee actually admired President Kennedy in his own reserved way," the memoir continues. "One day we discussed Kennedy's efforts to bring peace to the world and to end the Cold War. 'Great! Great!' exclaimed Lee. 'If he succeeds, he'll be the greatest president in the history of this country.' Kennedy's efforts to alleviate and to end segregation were also admired by Lee, who was sincerely and profoundly committed to complete integration and "saw in it the future of the United States." As he related Oswald's warm feeling toward Kennedy, he spoke equally of Oswald's torment over the unfairness of his military discharge downgrade. It explained Oswald's *"hatred of John Connally,"* the emigre wrote (emphasis mine).

After the assassination, de Mohrenschildt was the best witness on the question of what moved – and did not move – Lee Harvey Oswald, both politically and emotionally. Before the Warren Commission, he had been unhelpful, fearful of the consequences for his professional life and defensive about his relationship with the assassin. But as time went on, de Mohrenschildt was overcome with guilt and remorse for his trifling with Oswald.

In this critical period of Oswald's evolution toward violence, when Lee and Marina were having marital problems and had separated, Oswald and de Mohrenschildt saw each other frequently. In the manuscript that he gave to the House Select Committee on Assassinations in 1977, de Mohrenschildt painted a picture of Oswald very different from the conventional view. He touted Oswald's facility with the Russian language and even suggested that Oswald was reading the great Russian classics of Dostoyevsky, Pushkin, and Tolstoy in the original. He expressed his admiration for Oswald's independence and non-conformity, referring to him as "a remarkable fellow." And he told of how they engaged in almost continuous banter about both Russian and American politics, even reconstructing some of the jokes they traded.

De Mohrenschildt to Oswald: "Lee, you must have seen all over the world, the weak and poor are exploited everywhere by the powerful and the rich. Listen to this: Two dogs meet on the checkpoint between East and West Berlin. One dog is running away from capitalism, the other from communism. The capitalist dog asks, 'Why do you run away?'

And the [communist dog] answers: 'Because I can eat, but I can not bark.'

'And why do you run away?' [the communist dog] asks the [capitalist dog].

'Because if I bark, I cannot eat,' the capitalist dog answers."

Oswald countered with his own joke, one he had heard in Minsk. "As you know," he said to de Mohrenschildt, "Russians grab all they can from the satellite countries. So one day at a meeting of the Communist Party in Romania and with a Russian party official, one of the workers stands up and says, 'Comrade Secretary, may I ask you three questions?'

'Go ahead,' says the Party Secretary.

'I want to know what happened to our wheat, our petroleum, and our wine?'

'Well,' said the Secretary, 'it's a very complex question. I can not answer it immediately.'

A few months later, the workers hold the same type of meeting and another comrade raises his hands and says, 'Comrade Secretary, may I ask you four questions?'

'Shoot,' says the Secretary.

'I want to know what happened to our petroleum, our wine, our wheat, and also what happened to the comrade who asked the three questions some time ago?'"

At another point de Mohrenschildt tried to cheer up a bitter and melancholy Oswald with this tidbit about the meeting of four girls, French, English, American, and Russian.

"The French girl says, 'My lover will buy me a dress.' The English girl says, 'My husband promised to buy me a new coat.' The American girl brags: 'My boss will buy me a mink stole.' And the Russian girl responds: 'Girls, I am a prostitute also!'"

But such levity was not the norm. In general the conversation centered on heavier subjects like racial discrimination in America or Oswald's fear of the FBI and his disdain for religion or the stupidity of bureaucrats, both Russian and American. De Mohrenschildt toyed with Oswald in uneven intellectual games.

"Here the bureaucrats are nasty," Oswald said to de Mohrenschildt one day. "In the Soviet Union, they are naive and stupid."

"How in the hell did you get out of Russia so easily?" his mentor asked.

"I outsmarted those Russian bureaucrats," Oswald replied. "Man! They are just an amorphous bunch of people. They make a mistake and go to a concentration camp like a bunch of sheep."

De Mohrenschildt patronized Oswald mercilessly in these discussions, a behavior for which later he felt profoundly

guilty. And his baiting of Oswald went in concert with Marina's contempt. Once calling him a moron and a fool, she said,
"You're always thinking about politics instead about making
money. You act like a big shot."

By contrast, when the subject of JFK came up, according to de Mohrenschildt, Oswald was uniformly admiring:
"I showed him the president's picture on the cover of *Time*
magazine once, and Lee said, 'How handsome he looks, what
open and sincere features he has, and how different he looks
from the other ratty politicos. Look at the politicians here,
most of them,'" Oswald continued. "'They want to be praised
publically for their honest and good will. Connally, for example. In reality, they will do all the denigrating actions and yet
try to appear in a good light.'"

This was, de Mohrenschildt wrote, the first time that Oswald spoke of his "loathing" for Connally. In a later conversation, the touchy subject of his military discharge came up. "I
received an honorable discharge and then those bastards in
the navy changed it into an undesirable discharge, just because
I went to Russia and threw my passport in the face of the
American consul."

"Didn't they do it because you lied?" de Mohrenschildt
challenged. "You were supposed to go back to the States to
help your mother..."

"Oh, hell, that was just a crooked excuse," he replied sullen-
ly. "And Connally signed this undesirable discharge."

In 1964, George's daughter, Alexandra de Mohrenschildt,
also came before the Warren Commission. With this witness,
as with others who had known Oswald personally after his

repatriation, the commission probed Oswald's comparative attitude toward his eventual victims, looking for some insight that might explain his motive to murder. Alexandra was a good witness, for in the fall of 1962, she had been married to an engineer with liberal politics named Gary Taylor and had listened as Oswald and Taylor engaged in political discussion.

"Was President Kennedy ever mentioned in the course of the discussions between your husband and Lee?" the counsel asked.

"Never, never," Alexandra replied. "It was the governor of Texas who was mentioned mostly."

"Tell us about that."

"First you are going to have to tell me who the governor was."

"Connally."

"Connally...wasn't that the one that"

"That had been Secretary of the Navy."

"That had been Secretary of the Navy, was it? Well, for some reason, Lee just didn't like him. Don't know why, but he didn't like him."

"Would it refresh your recollection, that the subject of Governor Connolly arose in connection with something about Lee's discharge from the Marines?" the counsel prodded.

"I don't recall. Lee never spoke too much about why he left the Marines or anything like that. I don't know. Maybe it was the dishonorable discharge. I don't know. All I know is that it was something he didn't like to talk about. And there was a reason why he did not like Connally."

"Whatever the reason was, he didn't articulate the reason

particularly?"

"No, he just didn't like him."

"But you have the definite impression he had an aversion to Governor Connally?"

"Yes, but he never ever said a word about Kennedy."

"But he did have a definite aversion to Governor Connally as a person?"

"Yes."

In October, when Alexandra de Mohrenschildt was getting to know Oswald better and John Connally was in Dallas arguing for the continuation of the poll tax, Oswald had an experience that was becoming routine. The clerk at the Texas Employment Commission identified a good job opening in the photography department of a printing concern in Dallas called Jaggars-Chiles-Stovall. Before Oswald went over for his interview, the company had asked the employment commission clerk about Oswald's last place of employment and was told that he had recently been discharged from the Marines. When Oswald entered the Jaggars office, he made a good impression. He was presentably dressed and well-mannered. Almost immediately the subject of his military career came up, as the potential employer asked about his last place of work.

"The Marines," Oswald said brashly.

"Oh, yes-yes," the employer said. "Honorably discharged, of course," he added as a half-question, thinking he was being amusing.

"Oh, yes," Oswald replied with technical truthfulness.

Was this going to come up every time? His paranoia that his

lies might be discovered was intense. Later, the Jaggars-Chiles-Stovall man, John G. Graef, told the Warren Commission that it never occurred to him to check up on whether the applicant was telling the truth about the discharge, though it would have been perfectly easy to do so.

Oswald was to work six months at the Jaggars outfit. But his efficiency began to deteriorate in three months. He did not get along with the other employees. His behavior was unpredictable, his attitude unpleasant. Working in the close quarters of a photographic laboratory gave him claustrophobia, and this increased his churlishness.

Early in 1963, as his work at Jaggars declined, his thoughts drifted back to Russia. He seemed to block out the overwhelming negative feelings he had upon his departure. He began to talk to Marina about reentering the Soviet Union. If Russia had its spies and its drab, boring life-style, America with its capitalist moguls and its exploitation was wrong for him. Whatever it was, Soviet or American, the system was to blame. When Jaggars dismissed him in early April, Oswald brought it upon himself by flaunting a Soviet publication at work, once again attempting to turn failure into something noble: political martyrdom. On the day that he was fired, Oswald remarked that he hated capitalist exploitation and that the Jaggars firm had reaped a lot more from his labor than they had paid him in wages.

He had seen the end coming. Weeks before his dismissal he had secretly used the Jaggars facilities after hours to forge a new Marine Corps discharge and draft classification document in the name of Alek James Hidell.

Oswald forges a new discharge card in the name Alek James Hidell

Oswald's mail order rifle: Mannlicher-Carcano

It was the name he used to order his first weapon, a .39 caliber Smith and Wesson revolver, by mail, as well as his second, a high-powered Italian carbine called a Mannlicher-Carcano.

CHAPTER THREE:

The Turning

Three days into his first week of unemployment, on April 10, 1963, Lee Harvey Oswald became an assassin. His target was former Major-General Edwin Walker, an ultra right-wing reactionary, the darling of the John Birchers in Dallas, a West Point graduate who had distinguished himself in World War II when he commanded an elite Special Forces unit and had risen in the ranks to command a full division in Germany in the late 1950s. But Walker had resigned his commission in November 1961 after a speech in which he labeled Harry Truman and Eleanor Roosevelt as "pink." "I must be free from the power of little men who in the name of my country punish loyal service to it," he said grandly upon his departure. A month later, on December 4, 1961, he was featured on the cover of *Newsweek* magazine over the headline, "Thunder on the Right." The ex-general went on to run for governor of Texas in 1962 against John Connally, receiving over 200,000 votes. But his greater notoriety came in the fall of 1962 when he was jailed in Oxford, Mississippi for leading riots in protest against the admission of an African-American student, James Meredith, to Ole Miss. Charged with insurrection and jailed, he proclaimed upon his release:

"This is a conspiracy of the crucifixion by anti-Christ conspirators of the Supreme Court in their denial of prayer and their betrayal of the nation."

On an oval office tape recording at the time, JFK was heard to say, "Imagine that son of bitch having been the commander of a division up to a year ago. And the Army promoted him!"

As the attempted murder was later reconstructed, Oswald had crept into the upscale Turtle Creek neighborhood of Dallas where Walker lived and buried his rifle in an alley behind Walker's house. Returning three days later, he retrieved his rifle and took up his position by a lattice fence that bordered the general's backyard, waiting until after 9 p.m. for the music to begin at a worship service at a nearby Mormon Church. Walker sat in his study, sleeves rolled up, working on his taxes which were due in five days. Oswald rested his rifle on the lattice and squeezed off his round, missing Walker's head by about an inch, only because the bullet struck a wooden window frame and was deflected.

After my *Time* magazine cover story, November 25, 1988, on the assassination was published, I heard from William McMahon, a former reporter for CBS and the *Philadelphia Bulletin*. McMahon told me that after the Walker shooting, he had called the Dallas FBI and was informed that the FBI was not pursuing its investigation with any vigor. The Dallas agents had concluded that Walker had staged the assassination attempt himself to further his own political ambitions. McMahon always felt that this was yet another cruel turn of fate, for if the FBI had been more diligent in following up in the Walker shooting, Oswald would never have had a shot at Connally and Kennedy a few months later.

Lee Harvey Oswald had become a very dangerous man. Only one person, Marina Oswald, knew for sure about the attempt on General Walker. Only a few hours afterwards, he had come home sweating and exhausted and collapsed on their couch.

"I shot Walker," he blurted out.

"Is he dead?" she asked.

"I don't know," he answered.

In her narrow, isolated world, speaking only a few words of English, she knew nothing of American political figures, with the exception of the Kennedys. But when Lee Oswald confided in her, she understood his capability to kill for political reasons, and she was horrified. She saw what form his frustrations and failures were now taking.

Another person was soon to know about Oswald's attack. In the manuscript that was given to the House Select Committee on Assassinations in 1977, George de Mohrenschildt told of a visit he and his wife made to the Oswald apartment on Easter of that year. While being shown around the apartment, de Mohrenschildt's wife noticed a military-style rifle with a telescopic sight in the bedroom closet. This caused considerable excitement. Marina blurted out that her husband liked to shoot at leaves in the public park.

Peering wryly at Oswald, de Mohrenschildt said, "Did you

take a pot shot at General Walker, Lee?" Oswald seemed flummoxed and said nothing. "His facial expressions remained calm," de Mohrenschildt wrote, "he became a little paler...I think he mumbled something unintelligible." In relating this incident to the Warren Commission, Marina Oswald testified that de Mohrenschildt then said, "It's too bad you missed him."

This Easter visit was the last time de Mohrenschildt saw Oswald. But there would be a memento of the visit. Oswald would send his friend the now-famous picture of himself in the garden with the rifle in his right hand and a pistol strapped to his hip. On the back, Oswald wrote in Russian, "To my dear friend, George de Mohrenschildt, from Lee Oswald." Oswald or perhaps Marina – handwriting analysis was inconclusive – then added, "Hunter of Fascists. Ha! Ha! Ha!"De Mohrenschildt had forgotten about the picture until he found it fourteen years after the assassination. He referred to it as "a gift from the grave."

On the day in 1977 that an investigator from the House Select Committee on Assassination contacted him for questioning, George de Mohrenschildt committed suicide.

*　　*　　*　　*　　*

Two weeks after Easter, with Oswald still out of work and raging around their dingy apartment, Marina Oswald reacted.

On Sunday, April 21, 1963, the headline in the *Dallas News* read: CALLS FOR DECISION TO FORCE REDS OUT OF CUBA. It reported a strident speech which former Vice President Richard Nixon had made the previous day in Wash-

"Hunter of Fascists. Ha! Ha! Ha!"

ington, excoriating Kennedy for being "defensive" on Castro, demanding a "command decision" to remove the Soviets and calling for a redefinition of the manifest destiny of the Monroe Doctrine into a doctrine of liberation. Oswald laid the paper down and withdrew into an adjacent room. When he reemerged, he was dressed in a tie and white shirt. His pistol was shoved into his best gray pants.

"Where are you going?" Marina demanded.

"Nixon is coming to town. I want to go have a look."

"I know what your 'looks' mean," she said coldly, and then, thinking quickly, she enticed him into following her into the bathroom. Once he was inside, she slipped out and slammed the door, holding it tight with all her strength. For several minutes he pushed, and she held, and they shouted at one another, and Marina wept in terror. She pleaded with him not to go, to promise her he would never again go for one of his "looks." At last, emotionally spent, he agreed, and she let him out. In the days after this episode, later known as the "Nixon incident," Oswald became as torpid and unresponsive. Actually, Nixon was not in town at all, nor was he coming, and though Marina could not know it, Oswald did. He had said "Nixon" for its shock value: it was Nixon's picture that was on the front page of the Dallas paper. Since Nixon wasn't coming to Texas at all, the men of the Warren Commission dismissed the incident as having no "probative value."

It was *John Connally* who was coming.

The following day, the governor was scheduled to open a conference of space scientists at the Marriott Motor Inn in Dallas. The conference, held as the American Space program gloried in the success of the Mercury space missions, was widely advertised. Inside that Sunday paper which Oswald had read and then so ostentatiously laid down before he went to strap on his revolver was a story on Connally's San Jacinto Bay speech the day before. Connally had been at his manly, flag-waving best. In fact, he had waved three flags – that of Texas, that of America, and the bloody shirt of anticommunism. Before the soaring monument on the San Jacinto battlefield south of Houston, he said the spirit of the Texas Revolution made him stand "just a little taller, just a little stiffer to men like Castro and Khrushchev."

His speech was full of death imagery. The governor read from a missive written by the commander of the Alamo, Colonel William B. Travis, a letter well known to Texas schoolchildren: "The enemy has demanded a surrender. I answered the demand with a cannon shot, and our flag still waves proudly from the walls. Victory or death!" He quoted another letter, this from a fourteen-year-old boy at the tragic massacre at Goliad, also a place sacred to Texans: "They are going to shoot us in the back. Let us turn our faces and die like men." As for the Battle of San Jacinto, it had imparted "renewed hope in 1836 to all people who were under the foot of tyranny or who were threatened by tyranny. It gives equal hope today, when the foot of tyranny stands but ninety miles from our shore."

To Oswald, Connally's sentiments were no different from those of General Walker or Richard Nixon. All three represented the fascist edges of the despised monolith. In the first line of a grammatically tortured essay, written aboard ship on his return from Russia to the United States, he had wondered about capitalist and even "fascist" elements in America who "allways profess patriotism toward the land and the people, if not the government, although their movements must surely lead to the bitter destruction of all and everything … In these vieled, formless patriotic gestures, their is the obvious 'axe being ground' by the invested interests of the sponsors of there expensive undertaking."

In Oswald's jangled kaleidoscope, Connally, Nixon, and

Walker were interchangeable parts of the radical right. But Connally – his head shot suspended and grinning from a Texas star – inhabited a special place.

Six months before his San Jacinto speech, on October 5, 1962, the gubernatorial candidate made a swing through Dallas for two highly publicized campaign speeches. It was the same day Oswald was laid off at the welding company. Then, exactly two weeks after he lost his job at Jaggars-Chiles-Stovall, and as he was having no luck finding another job, Connally turned up again in Dallas. In Oswald's deck of fantasies, paranoias, and delusions, Connally seemed to be the deadly jack of spades. When the knave's face turned up, bad things happened.

If in April 1963, Oswald became a hunter of fascists, it is hard to imagine President John F. Kennedy becoming his quarry. The political topics that engaged Oswald's passion and his rage were civil rights, disarmament with the Soviet Union, and Cuba. Upon the first two, Kennedy acted as Oswald would have approved in the term preceding November 22, 1963, and upon the third, two years after his disaster at the Bay of Pigs, Kennedy had become a voice of moderation.

In October 1962, when Oswald lost his first job, Kennedy was dealing with the riots at Ole Miss and with the lurid arch-segregationist Ross Barnett. Meanwhile, Oswald's first target, General Walker, who had gone to Ole Miss, was arrested by Kennedy's federal troops for inciting to riot, and upon his release was welcomed back triumphantly to Dallas.

In the spring of 1963, after Oswald took off for New Orleans to find work, Kennedy was grappling with the massive resistance of George Wallace and the police dogs of Bull Connor in Birmingham and was sending in federal troops to protect African-Americans there. On June 10, Kennedy gave his famous speech on disarmament at American University. In it, the president was generous about the Russian people, expressing sentiments with which Oswald would agree:

"No government or social system is so evil that its people must be considered as lacking in virtue," Kennedy said. "As Americans, we find Communism profoundly repugnant as a negation of personal freedom and dignity. But we must still hail the Russian people for their many achievements – in science and space, in economic and industrial growth, in culture and in acts of courage." At American University, Kennedy took the occasion to announce the opening of high-level talks between Britain, the United States, and the Soviet Union on a limited nuclear test ban treaty. Throughout the summer, the hopeful possibility of an accord dominated the news. On July 20, a draft agreement was concluded – it was the first effort to bring nuclear weapons under international control in the eighteen years of the nuclear age.

In late July, both Connally and Oswald also made significant and revealing public appearances. On July 19, Connally traveled to Miami for the national governors' conference, armed with all the high-flown, defiant rhetoric of Colonel Travis at the Alamo. In this case, however, the crumbling walls were the Southern laws of segregation, which were under frontal attack from Kennedy and the civil rights leaders. Of the public accommodation sections of Kennedy's integration plan, Connally said:

"They would be laws which in my judgment, would strike at the very foundation of one of our most cherished freedoms: the right to own and manage civil property."

The governor sweetened his speech with praise of moderation and voluntary desegregation, with talk of education and economic opportunity as the solution to racism, with sympathy for the hard-pressed national leadership. But he positioned himself and his state foursquare in the Southern camp, making the difference between himself and George Wallace and Ross Barnett only a matter of degree, tone, and emphasis. Interestingly, Lyndon Johnson, who came from the same Texas soil, had now made the leap ahead of his region. Admittedly, it was easier for Johnson – he was a national rather than a regional figure now – and he was supposed to toe the administration's line. But Johnson's words went farther than mere fealty to the boss. In his opening address to the governors' conference, he opened a gap between himself and his constituency in the audience: "Our foremost challenge is to face and dispose of the problem of human rights which has burdened and compromised our society for a hundred years: the problem of inequality of our Negro citizens."

On July 27, a few days after the conference, Lee Harvey Oswald also made a speech. From New Orleans, he ventured to Mobile, Alabama, a town whose hardened Dixie attitude toward race was made all the more impenetrable by its romance with Confederate chivalry, and whose leading citizens – many of them at least – subscribed to the view their governor had expressed to the U.S. Senate Commerce Committee only a few days earlier: that the civil rights movement was led by Communists and directed from Moscow. Oswald had a cousin who was studying to be a Jesuit priest at Spring Hill College and had invited Oswald to speak to the Jesuit scholastics about his experiences in Russia. This was unquestionably the most dignified moment in the life of Lee Harvey Oswald. He was to be part of a lecture series, which included pastors from other faiths as well as other personages who had something significant to say, and he could be sure that the earnest novitiates would treat him with respect and openness.

He made a good impression. The audiences, including senior priests, found him articulate and informative, if somewhat nervous and humorless. Their expectation that they might derive a clearer view of life in the Soviet Union from this recent resident than from official reports seems to have been fulfilled. He engaged their interests immediately with a personal narrative of his time in the Minsk factory and then expressed his central belief: he disliked capitalism because of its exploitation of the poor. He had been disillusioned by Russian Communism because of the gap between Marxist theory and Soviet reality.

"Capitalism doesn't work. Communism doesn't work. In the middle is socialism and that doesn't work either," he said.

If Oswald was a crackpot, the scholastics did not perceive it. They took him seriously, plying him with a series of questions afterwards. Far from intimidated, Oswald answered adroitly, succinctly, and without petulance.

"What impressed you most about Russia?" someone asked.

"The care that the state provides everyone," he replied. "If a man gets sick, no matter what his status is, how poor he is,

the state will take care of him....If the Negroes in the United
States knew it was so good in Russia, they'd want to go there."

That was as abrasive as he got. In the decisive summer
of 1963 in Alabama, only a few weeks after Medgar Evers
had been assassinated in neighboring Mississippi, and a few
weeks before the bombing in the 16th Street Baptist Church
in Birmingham, where four small girls were murdered, the
remark was scarcely revolutionary, but it showed something
about Oswald's political passions: the black man and the little man were those with whom he identified. The country
was already preparing for the great march on Washington in
a few weeks, when Martin Luther King, Jr. would speak of
his dream. Southern governors, including Connally, warned
of disruptions the march might bring. Kennedy, on the other
hand, told the press conference in July that he hoped leaders
in government, in business, and in labor would do something
about the fundamental problem that had led to the demonstration.

Marina Oswald was to say later that her husband never
uttered a harsh or angry word against Kennedy. If he had any
negative emotion, it was envy. In the year before the assassination, Oswald avidly read William Manchester's flattering
biography of Kennedy, *Portrait of a President,* and Kennedy's
Profiles in Courage. He had become fascinated by the lives of
great men, and to Marina, he predicted that Kennedy would
be "prime minister" of America in twenty years. In the spring
and summer of 1964, Marina Oswald was pregnant again, as
was Mrs. Kennedy, and Marina followed the course of Mrs.
Kennedy's term keenly. In April 1963, the Oswalds watched

the television report of the Kennedys in Palm Beach together
to see if Mrs. Kennedy was showing signs of her pregnan-
cy. While later testimony suggested Lee Oswald harbored
a mild resentment of Kennedy's wealth, he told Marina that
JFK was qualified to be president and deserved to be president. By the summer, Marina would flip through magazines
looking for pictures of Kennedy. When she found one, she
would demand that Lee translate the accompanying article,
which he did.

*In all the literature that has been generated by the assassi-
nation of John F. Kennedy, nowhere can there be found a single
reference to any personal animosity that Oswald felt toward the
president.* Indeed, the reverse is true. To believe that John F.
Kennedy, as the liberal president of the United States and the
humane leader of the free world, was Oswald's prime target, as
the Warren Commission did, one must believe that between
the attack on Walker in April and the killing of Kennedy in
November, Oswald's pathology of violence broadened into a
cosmology of direct violent action against the highest authority. The Warren Commission reasoned that from April to November, Oswald moved from ire against right-wing figures to
hatred of all figures of authority generally, regardless of their
positions toward the concerns that moved Oswald: civil lib-
erties, regard for the working man, and accommodation with
the Soviet Union.

The treatment of Oswald's motive for the assassination by
both the Warren Commission in 1964 and the House Assassinations Committee in 1977 is woefully inadequate. The
Warren Commission retreated into vague conclusions, refer-

ring to Oswald's "overriding hostility to his environment," and suggesting that the assassin was searching for "a place in history – a role as the 'great man' who would be recognized as having been in advance of his times." It also ascribed a "commitment to Marxism" as having played part in his motivation. It was as if the powerbrokers of Washington, who comprised the Warren Commission – Chief Justice Earl Warren, CIA director Allen Dulles, presidential advisor John J. McCloy, senators John Sherman Cooper and Richard Russell, and House leaders Hale Boggs and Gerald Ford – had to assign to Oswald a political motive as grand and horrendous as the crime itself. Oswald's motive, as a committed Marxist, was to bring down the U.S. government by decapitating its head, they argued. That was an intellectual motive they could relate to. But Oswald's real motive was more the province of novelists and psychologists than Washington insiders.

The House Assassinations Committee took a laundry-list approach to the motive, as it acknowledged: "Finding a possible motive for Oswald's having assassinated President Kennedy was one of the most difficult issues the Warren Commissioned faced." The House Committee fell back on "politics" as the prime driver of Oswald's action: "It seems reasonable to conclude that the best single explanation for the assassination was his conception of political action, rooted in his twisted ideological view of himself and the world around him."

This question lingers: Could Lee Harvey Oswald have been an agent of either state violence or mob violence? With such barely formed ideas, such grandiosity, such determined independence, Oswald was scarcely a good prospect to be re-

cruited as an assassin by a foreign state or by the Mafia. If
Cuba, the Soviet Union, or a big-time mobster had wanted to
assassinate an American president, they had far more reliable
instruments of violence than Oswald. Lee Harvey Oswald
was no jackal.

Shortly before his own speech in Mobile, Oswald had listened approvingly with Marina as the president announced
the nuclear test ban treaty. Even on the subject of Cuba, which
in New Orleans Oswald had taken up as the latest cause to
draw attention to himself, the assassin gave Kennedy the benefit of the doubt. To Marina he remarked that Kennedy was
inclined toward the softer attitude regarding Cuba than many
on the American political scene.

In the few months before Kennedy went to Dallas in November, his statements on Castro were boilerplate. In Florida
on November 18, only four days before his death, the president's rhetoric about Castro was far from inflammatory. The
administration's efforts "to isolate the virus of Communism"
had met with success, Kennedy thought, and Castro, once a
formidable symbol of revolution, had faded. Kennedy even
berated those stale naysayers who continued to complain
about Castro and blamed all the hemisphere's problems on
Communism or on right-wing generals. "The harsh facts of
poverty and social justice will not yield easily to promises or
good will," the president said.

Even if one accepts Oswald's concern for Cuba as sincere
and deeply felt, is it conceivable that Kennedy's statements on
Cuba in the latter part of 1963 could have become the motive
for assassination? The Warren Commission thought so. Its

members never considered the difference between benign and violent political action, for that moved the question from the familiar turf of politics to the unfamiliar area of emotion and psychology. They were unconcerned to untwist Oswald's "twisted ideological view." By simply labeling it *twisted*, they abrogated their responsibility to understand and then to explain.

* * * * *

On July 25, 1963, Oswald received the decision of the Navy Discharge Review Board. "It is the decision of the Board that no change, correction or modification is warranted in your discharge."

The background rationale cited Oswald's attempt to renounce citizenship "and become a permanent citizen of the Soviet Union," and the adverse publicity about his behavior that "had brought discredit to the Marine Corps." Therefore, he had proved himself unfit for retention in the naval service. In Oswald's demented psychology, his situation was now clarified.

A few weeks after the Board's letter, Oswald was back in New Orleans, and there, he finally got to be a big shot…briefly. Posting as the New Orleans secretary of a group called Fair Play for Cuba, he began distributing literature on the streets. The police quickly noticed this, and he was arrested for trespassing. The local news picked up the story, and the coverage caught the attention of a local broadcaster named William Stuckey. Stuckey had a radio program on the local station called "Latin Listening Post." Tracking the leafleteer

DEPARTMENT OF THE NAVY
NAVY DISCHARGE REVIEW BOARD
WASHINGTON 25, D. C.

IN REPLY REFER TO
EXOS:QB(33)
JAP:cjo

Commission Exhibit No. 1092

JUL 25 1963

Mr. Lee H. Oswald
P. O. Box 30061
New Orleans, La.

Dear Mr. Oswald:

    The review of your discharge has been completed in accordance with the regulations governing the procedures of this Board. Careful consideration was given to the evidence presented in your behalf as well as that contained in your official records. The Secretary of the Navy has reviewed the proceedings of the Board.

    It is the decision that no change, correction or modification is warranted in your discharge.

Sincerely yours,

D. W. BOWMAN
Captain, USN
President
Navy Discharge Review Board

REGISTERED

Encls: Original Discharge Certificate.
      Two (2) letters dated 31 Jan 1962, 13 Nov 1961.
      Information on Reenlistment

NAVEXOS 1900/1 (REV. 11-62)

822330

Finality

The service record of petitioner shows that he was discharged as unfit for good and sufficient reasons. This was based on reliable information which indicated that he had renounced his U.S. citizenship with the intentions of becoming a permanent citizen of the Union of Soviet Socialist Republics. Further, that petitioner brought discredit to the Marine Corps through adverse newspaper publicity, which was generated by the foregoing action, and had thereby, in the opinion of his commanding officer, proved himself unfit for retention in the naval service.

Navy Discharge Review Board decision, July 10th, 1963

down at his address, he got Oswald on tape. In speaking about his background, Oswald mentioned his honorable discharge from the Marines, but neglected to mention its change in status. He spoke of his home base in Dallas, but did not mention his three years in Russia. After the interview was broadcast on August 17, Stuckey got a few calls from anti-Communist and anti-Cuban sources that scolded Stuckey for not knowing the full story. So Stuckey promptly arranged for a second program in which several anti-Communist activists in New Orleans would confront Oswald.

The second program on August 21 turned into an interrogation. Yes, Oswald admitted, he had lived in Russia for three years. Yes, he was a Marxist. "Is this a Fair Play for Cuba or Fair Play for Russia Committee?" he was asked. "This is a very provocative question," Oswald retorted bravely. "I don't think it requires an answer."

"How many people do you have in your Committee here in New Orleans?"

"As Secretary of the Fair Play for Cuba Committee, I can not reveal that."

"You at one time asked to renounce your citizenship and become a Soviet citizen. Is that correct?"

"I don't think that has any import to this discussion."

"Are you a communist?"

"I am a Marxist."

"What's the difference?"

"The difference is, as I have said, a very great difference. Many parties, many countries are based on Marxism. Many countries such as Great Britain display very socialistic aspects or characteristics. I might point to the socialized medicine of Britain…"

And so it went. Oswald was in trouble, and after the program, from his dejected state, he seemed to know it. Lee Harvey Oswald could now have no illusions. Another arrest had been added to his record. And in a very public way, his Marxism, his attempt to renounce his American citizenship, and his political activity for a far-left group were exposed. Already paranoid of the FBI, as he confessed to de Mohrenshildt, he could hardly have been surprised that these events attracted the Bureau's attention.

*   *   *   *   *

Several other facts are worth noting about this period in the few months before November 1963. It seems that assassination was in the wind in America, both in popular culture and in reality. In December 1962, the assassination film, *The Manchurian Candidate*, had played for over a month in Dallas, and it seems highly probable that Oswald had seen it. Marina Oswald testified that he would often go to the movies alone, and the Palace Theater downtown was not far from where he worked. Medgar Evers, the great Mississippi civil rights leader, was assassinated in July. Shortly before their child was born in October 1963, Marina Oswald would testify to the Warren Commission, the couple watched a rerun of a 1949 John Huston film called *We Were Strangers*. The plot focuses on a group of desperate revolutionaries who were intent to overthrow the corrupt Cuban government by assassinating the dictator and all his lackeys at a state funeral. Indeed, Marina testified, Oswald watched the movie twice over the weekend of October 12-13. This was only two days before Oswald got his job at the Texas Book Depository with a salary of $50 per week.

At issue is Oswald's will to murder. Was it, at its core, emotional or intellectual? Toward Connally, he had a simple, visceral grudge – a grudge that engaged his emotions, his anger, and his oceanic resentment. The governor's smiling face peering out and tormenting Oswald in the middle of the Texas star personalized his frustrations and setbacks. Grafted onto that central hatred in 1963 were other factors: his pose as a Marxist and a political activist, the failure of his assassination attempt on General Walker, the finality of the Navy Discharge Review Board in July, the coverage that summer of the Medgar Evers killing, the grand fantasy of being someone important who would be remembered as a figure of history, the influence of the Hollywood movies. His obsession with Connally was joined with his feeling of being wronged. It was a powerful and dangerous combination.

But what investigators know is that with crime, especially political crime, there must be not only emotional motive but also access. It was not until November 19 that the precise route of the presidential motorcade was published in the *Dallas Times Herald*. Only then did Oswald know for sure that Governor Connally and President John F. Kennedy would be passing directly under his window at the Texas Book Depository in Dealey Plaza.

The members of the Warren Commission and later the House Committee on Assassinations may have been reluctant to attempt to untangle Oswald's psychology, but Marina, who knew his feelings best, offered important testimony on that subject. In each of the three times she testified before the Warren Commission, Marina Oswald revealed, in greater and more convincing detail, important episodes she had either forgotten or repressed, providing more convincing explanations for her husband's state of mind. In her first appearance, as the commission's very first witness only six weeks after the assassination, she regretfully acknowledged that she now accepted her husband as the president's murderer. Why had he done it? For good reasons or bad, she replied, her husband wanted to become a memorable figure of history. The commission seized upon this as a simple, comprehensible, and salable motive, and never let go of it.

In her second appearance, in June 1964, she suddenly remembered the "Nixon incident," with her husband shouting at her through the bathroom door, "You always get in my way!" but the commission promptly dismissed the entire matter as insubstantial.

Her third appearance took place in Dallas only three weeks before the Warren Commission Report was released, when its conclusions were already set in stone. It was no time to reopen a Pandora's box of motives. Nevertheless, as Congressman Hale Boggs of Louisiana questioned her sharply, she said, seemingly out of thin air:

"I feel in my own mind that Lee did not have President Kennedy as a prime target when he assassinated him."

"Well, who was it?" Boggs asked, almost languorously.

"I think it was Connally," she replied. "That's my personal opinion – that he perhaps was shooting at Governor Connally, the governor of Texas."

This was not what they wanted to hear, and Senator Richard Russell jumped on her.

"Why do you think he would shoot *him*?"

"I feel that the reason that he had Connally in his mind was on account of his discharge from the Marines and various letters they exchanged between the Marine Corps and the governor's office, but actually, I didn't think that he had any idea concerning President Kennedy."

"Well, did he ever express any hostility toward Governor Connally?" Boggs asked.

"He never expressed that to me – his displeasure or hatred of Connally," she said, holding her ground, for he seems to have exposed so little of his political nature to her. "I feel that there could have been some connection, due to the fact that Lee was dishonorably discharged from the corps. That's my personal opinion."

Instead of pursuing this new and highly significant tack or calmly attempting to elicit more from her, Boggs and Russell proceeded to browbeat the widow with the inconsistency of this with her prior testimony, and they quickly left the subject altogether. No reference to it whatever appears in their final report because, of course, the final report was already written.

It would be fourteen years before an additional, decisive detail was added to this thorny question of motive. In 1978, Marina Oswald testified before the House Assassinations Committee. Almost offhandedly, assigning no particular significance to it herself and finding that the politicians of the House were no more interested than the Warren Commission had been, she told of how Connally's brush-off letter in February 1962 was the origin of the grudge, and of how it had arrived at their Minsk apartment in the big, white envelope whose front flaunted the large smiling face of John Connally, advertising his candidacy for governor of Texas.

"I stand by my testimony to the Warren Commission," she said.

CHAPTER FOUR:

Roads Taken Reluctantly

The origin of President John F. Kennedy's trip to Texas in November 1963 is a subject that has passed through the prism of shame and collective guilt and emerged as a blur. With its terrible result, it appears that nobody really wanted the trip. JFK was irritated to have to make it. John Connally had stalled it and argued against it, and when he could no longer resist it, had wanted Dallas eliminated from the itinerary. It was laid on without Lyndon Johnson's counsel, and when the vice president heard about the final arrangements, he resented his exclusion. And Senator Yarborough, the liberal foil to Connally and the fourth player in the political prelude to tragedy, was merely bracing himself against the fierce political winds that were swirling around him. Yarborough was a flowery, old-fashioned former colonel in the U.S. Army who went by the nickname of Raff and who had learned his liberalism in the wheat fields of Oklahoma and in the boom oil fields around Bolger, Texas.

Even the purpose of the trip remains in dispute. Was Kennedy going primarily to raise money for his 1964 campaign? Was he going to heal the rift between the liberal and conservative factions of the Texas Democratic party represented by Yarborough and Connally? Was he going to shore up a shaky Connally governorship? Did Lyndon Johnson need the presidential trip to bolster his own standing and ensure that he would remain on the ticket the next year? The survivors of Elm Street agree on one thing in speaking later to history: no one was to blame. Nor is there value in applying vague standards of moral or metaphysical guilt for the tragedy, although those standards were liberally applied in its aftermath, especially by the city of Dallas, which was tormented then – and still is – over whether its atmosphere of hostility and even hate for the Kennedys influenced Lee Harvey Oswald in any way.

That said, the presidential trip to Texas was an unmitigated political disaster, even before the presidential motorcade made its fateful turn from Houston Street onto Elm Street. Even if there had been no shooting, it would have reverberated for weeks and probably months as an embarrassment to all involved. It was politics at its least elevating.

By John Connally's account, President Kennedy had been pushing for more than a year and a half to come to Texas, extending back to a time even before Connally became governor. The state of Texas, whose native son was vice presidential and which had provided the margin of victory in 1960, had contributed virtually nothing to the national Democratic party since his election, and the party labored under a $4 million debt. Kennedy was disgruntled. The flow of "oil" into the tanks of the national party was long overdue. If the president was irritated at having to travel to Texas, his irritation lay in the necessity of the president himself having to unclog the pipes when his vice president or a strong governor should have been able to handle the job without him.

Connally has written that he held off a presidential trip to his state as long as he could, but in any event, he was in no position to help or to host until he became governor in January. He has also written that his state recognized its financial obligation to the national party and that it would have discharged it... eventually. But his distance from the national administration and his disagreement with the essence of the Kennedy program indicate that he would have stalled on that responsibility as long as he could.

Through the spring, Connally was preoccupied with getting his first programs through the state legislature, so it wasn't until June that serious planning finally began, with Kennedy again taking the initiative. Early in the month, Kennedy undertook a whirlwind Western swing that included commencement addresses at the Air Force Academy and in San Diego, and speeches in Honolulu before he returned to Washington for his remarkable address on disarmament on June 10. After his address to the Air Force cadets, he touched down briefly in El Paso, where he was met by Governor Connally and Vice President Johnson. After an open-air motorcade, much like the one later in Dallas, the three repaired to the Cortez Hotel downtown to talk politics. As Connally remembered the meeting, the president got right to the point, even before the governor could take a chair.

"Well, Lyndon," Kennedy said with a twinkle, "do you think we're *ever* going to have that fundraising affair in Texas?"

"You have the governor here, Mr. President. Maybe *now* you can get a commitment from him."

It was a trap Connally could not wriggle out of. As he would put it later, his string had run out. "Fine, Mr. President. Let's start planning your trip," he said with resignation.

The symbolic significance of Texas and Massachusetts was clearly important to both Kennedy and Johnson. They represented the Boston-Austin axis of the administration, and much ballyhoo had been made of that at the 1960 convention. It was not long into the conversation before Kennedy gave voice to it again.

"If we don't raise funds in any other state, I want to do so in Massachusetts and in Texas," he said. "If we don't carry any other state next year, I want to carry Texas and Massachusetts."

For Kennedy and Johnson, that was a relatively straightforward and sentimental proposition, but it was not so simple for Connally. In a state with two-year terms for the governor, he too faced election the following year, and his chances for reelection did not lie in associating himself with the national administration and its goals. In the culture of Kennedy America, where grace and elegance and good looks counted for much, Connally had derived considerable mileage from the illusion that he was a Texas version of the Kennedys. But his politics were as conservative as those of most national Republicans in 1952 and 1956, and Texas had just put the Republican John Tower in the Senate. Connally was being asked to spend his political credit for the national liberals, when his constituents loathed the spirit of the Kennedy administration more than the governor himself did.

Moreover, with his election to the governorship, Connally had, at long last, emerged somewhat from the shadow of Lyndon Johnson and was finally becoming something of his own man. He was determined to nurture a clear identity, separate and distinct from both Johnson and Kennedy. Putting himself out for their cause would only improve the fortunes of his archrival in Texas, Senator Ralph Yarborough. Connally detested Yarborough and Yarborough despised Connally, and their mutual contempt extended back to the fierce fights between Texas liberals and conservatives in the mid-1950s.

For Connally the proposal was fraught with political risk. Kennedy plowed on undaunted, apparently insensitive to Connally's problem. He proposed not one political fundraiser, but four, and Connally gulped in disbelief. This was not so much a political incursion as a full-scale invasion. The president thought dinners in Houston, San Antonio, Fort Worth, and Dallas were about right. Whether Kennedy made this suggestion seriously, or simply to test Connally's loyalty, is unclear. He was too good a politician not to understand that four political dinners in one visit would create the unseemly impression of a president come only to milk the wealth of the state. But Kennedy forged ahead. Maybe Lyndon Johnson's birthday, August 27, would provide the right pretext for the political fundraisers. To the Texans, this too was a lousy idea. Johnson said nothing, his eyes hooded and downcast.

"Well, Mr. President, I would like to think about that,"

Connally stalled. "You know my feelings for the vice president. His birthday is always a time for celebration, but the
very people you want to reach aren't likely to be here. Texas
gets mighty hot in August. It's the worst month of the year
to have a fund-raising affair… for anybody. People are not
interested in politics during the dog days, and I think it would
be a serious mistake to come then."

"If you don't like that date, what date do you like?" Kennedy shot back. Connally hedged, but the president would
not have it. The easy bantering was done. "Let's get on with
it," he said in a clipped voice. "We've been talking about this
for a year and a half or more. Let's get an agreement about
what we're going to do and get together and start making our
plans."

No agreement was forged that night in El Paso, only the
promise by Connally to come up with a plan. Lyndon Johnson badgered the governor from time to time through the
summer. On one call, he said again that the president wanted
four or five fundraisers.

"That's a mistake," Connally snapped.

"Well, that is what he wants, and you had better be prepared to do it, or better be prepared to give him a real good
reason why you can't do it."

Johnson might have gotten away with that tactic in his
congressional office in 1939, but not now.

"All right, I will work out something," Connally replied
stiffly, "and be back in touch with you."

In due course, after talking with state legislators and his
men in the party, Connally did come up with a plan: one po-

litical dinner, rather than four, to be held in Austin in the fall. If the president wanted to visit other Texas cities, those stops should be dignified, presidential, and essentially nonpolitical. One fundraiser, if properly organized, could raise as much money as four anyway, the governor felt, and Austin was the one enclave in Texas where Democrats of all persuasions could come without feeling themselves to be on somebody else's high ground.

The subject languished until the fall, and Connally preferred that it languish indefinitely. In mid-September, however, the White House began to push the governor for the final plan. A meeting with the president was set for October 3.

*　　*　　*　　*　　*

On September 25, Lee Harvey Oswald left New Orleans for Mexico City, where his destination was the Cuban embassy. He wanted to explore the possibility of returning to Russia. His inability to fit into American society had evidently made him forget how the Communist bureaucrats could cruelly buffet him. But in Mexico City, those memories would return in a rush, as the Cuban and Soviet embassies squashed any dream he may have had of a heroic return. They scarcely let him in the front door. Oswald's trip to Mexico was such a blow that it makes the claim absurd that, two months later, his impulse to murder had the motive of promoting the Cuban or Soviet cause.

His preoccupations at home were mundane, not geopolitical. Since August, he had ceased to search for gainful employment; at this point, it had become too hard and too embarrassing. That he had been arrested in New Orleans for distributing Fair Play for Cuba Committee pamphlets – in short, for leftist activity – made him even less employable than he had been before. But the root of his job troubles lay in the downgraded military discharge. If that could have been corrected, things might be different, but the Navy had made its final decision.

The Warren Commission was to receive persuasive testimony that on his way to Mexico City, Oswald stopped for an afternoon in Austin. He came to see Governor Connally. There he was seen having lunch at Trek's Restaurant before he went to the state capitol, to see again if Connally wouldn't intervene for him over his discharge. Perhaps in person the governor would be more responsive. There is no record of Oswald's visit, because this time Oswald got his brush-off orally. He was told that the governor did not handle military matters. Oswald was directed to the Selective Service. There he was served by a clerk named Lee Dannelly, who later remembered him well. She remembered him partly because he was so ugly; in fact, he was the ugliest man she had ever seen, but Dannelly had other reasons to remember Oswald. He gave his name as Harvey Oswald, and she searched for it without success in the available files. After he explained the downgrade of his discharge, he said he had been informed that if he lived an "upright" life for two years, he could appeal the status again. The undesirable discharge was making it impossible for him to get a good job, he told her, and it was embarrassing to his family.

This was scarcely a fleeting encounter. Oswald was with

the clerk for about thirty minutes. The end result was the same as it had been since he got his first reply from Connally. He was told to write to a new address far away, to another agency, about another form, a different procedure, a different board of appeals.

*   *   *   *   *

Before he went to Washington to see President Kennedy, Connally went to Dallas. He was the reluctant captain, ordered by his admiral to do what he considered to be unwise. As a good sailor, he would swallow his pride, go along with the plan. Since he could see no alternative, he would put the best face on it for the good of Old Glory. A captain, he told his business supporters, could scarcely bar the admiral from boarding the ship. By this stance, he separated himself from the president, without disobeying him. In Dallas, he met with the power elite: the chairman of the Dallas Citizens Council, which had controlled Dallas politics for forty years; the president of the Chamber of Commerce; the head of the Mercantile, the oldest bank in Dallas; and executives from the two Dallas newspapers. These were Connally's kind of folks, and in such meetings he was at his best.

Dallas, Texas, as represented by the men in Connally's meeting, was deeply concerned about its image. It wanted to be known as bursting with vitality, a place of limitless opportunity and big dreams, where the myth of Texas wealth was a palpable reality. It was, however, increasingly being portrayed as "a leading center of hate and hysteria" in America. The image-makers fretted at how people on the outside associated their city with its radical fringe, and yet that fringe, in the past few years, had taken a few memorable actions that were hard to play down. There was the "spitting incident" of November 4, 1960 when an unruly, ugly crowd jostled and heckled candidate Lyndon and Lady Bird Johnson in the lobby of the Adolphus Hotel, and a similar incident against Adlai Stevenson two weeks after Connally came to Dallas to meet with the business establishment.

The Stevenson episode did not redound to Connally's credit. The U.N. ambassador had come to Texas to give a speech in connection with the United Nations on October 24. When the right-wing hotheads made a fuss about Stevenson's appearance, Connally pandered to them by declaring October 24 also to be United States Day in Texas. With this apparent official sanction, a mob surrounded Stevenson after his speech, spat upon him, and bonked him on the head with a placard.

Ostensibly, Connally was horrified. Immediately, he issued a statement to the press decrying the incident and wrote Stevenson a personal note of apology. On November 1, Stevenson replied, thanking the governor for his note and asserting that, but for a "minute handful," his reception in Dallas had been warm.

"After this incident, I feel all the more confident that the President's visit to Texas will be gratifying to you as well as to him!" Stevenson wrote.

Two weeks later, on November 13, only nine days before the Dallas motorcade, Connally replied: "Of course as Governor of Texas, I was distressed by what occurred, but extremely proud of you and the way you handled the entire matter, both at the time and later in the press. Your graciousness is deeply appreciated. We are looking forward to the President's visit and, like you, I am confident that it will be both pleasant and rewarding."

(The U.N. ambassador was handed this letter a few minutes after he had heard the news of the shooting in Dallas on November 22.)

If Dallas despised Johnson and Stevenson, it loved John Connally. He was their glamorous man on horseback, fitting perfectly Dallas' image of how a leader should look, talk, and act. In turn, Connally liked the way Dallas practiced politics. The city chose its mayor as if it were a pure oligarchy. The businessmen determined the candidate, and the citizens ratified their choice.

Now, at the Adolphus Hotel, Connally virtually apologized to the Dallas leadership for the president's insistence on coming to Texas and to Dallas. Since he could not prevent it altogether, he could at least prevent it from being a liberal love fest.

"I don't intend to default to the liberals," Connally told the group. "I've got to have a nonpolitical body to represent Dallas, and you gentlemen are it, by your associations."

Connally was, however, sensitive to the concerns of his listeners about the reputation of Dallas and he worried that some embarrassment would befall the president there. Regardless of the liberal-conservative divide, any discourtesy would reflect badly on Dallas and on the state, and be an embarrassment to Connally, personally, as the president's official host. Connally left the meeting for Washington to argue that Dallas should be reconsidered as a stop in the president's itinerary.

The news of the Dallas visit broke in the Dallas paper on September 26, and others were considerably more fearful of the stop than Connally. Chief among them was Byron Skelton, the courtly national committeeman from northeast Texas. Since May, Skelton had been writing letters to the Texas contingent in the White House about a presidential trip to Texas, alternating enthusiasm and irritation, but he had been excluded from the planning of the trip, and so everything he wrote and said subsequently was dismissed as sour grapes. The Dallas stop worried Skelton, and he worried specifically for the safety of the president. He noted General Walker's taunts – that President Kennedy was a menace to the free world – which had been prominently reported in the *Dallas Morning News*. As far as he was concerned, the paper had been writing stories for years that were tailor-made to stir up an unbalanced person.

In Washington, Senator William Fulbright of Arkansas was a grim-faced Cassandra. His distrust and downright fear of Dallas went back to the early 1950s, when his had been the sole vote in the U.S. Senate against appropriating for Senator McCarthy's red-scare campaign, and Dallas had generated a major proportion of the hate mail that followed. The *Dallas Morning News* had made Fulbright its regular whipping boy, especially when he became Chairman of the Senate Foreign Relations Committee, charging him with being a "red louse" and unrepresentative of his state. The reactionary Hunts of

Dallas had poured a pot of money into unsuccessful campaigns to defeat him. To Fulbright, Dallas was a *physically* dangerous place, and he predicted that, given the current environment, Kennedy would suffer some abuse.

On October 3, the day before the president met with Connally for the first planning, Fulbright had accompanied Kennedy to Arkansas for the dedication of the Greers Ferry Dam in Herber Springs and for a rousing speech about the rising New South at the state fairgrounds in Little Rock. Repeatedly along the way, Fulbright returned to the subject of Dallas, warning the president not to go there.

Despite the warnings and controversy, the president seemed unconcerned. There was no way he could make a swing of major Texas cities without going to Dallas. That Dallas had voted against him in 1960 hardly made the city unique. As for demonstrations, he had a theory. Generally, the nasty characters in any given American city numbered no more than fifty individuals, and what Dallas could muster would be no nastier than what the fringe might stage anywhere else. When the worrywarts brought up the Johnson episode at the Baker Hotel, Kennedy reminded them that during the same campaign of 1960, he too had gone to Dallas and had had one of the more courteous receptions of the entire campaign.

Before Connally saw the president, he ventured to Capitol Hill for a breakfast meeting with the Texas congressional delegation. In the Speaker's Room, the governor's task was almost schoolmarmish: he needed to assign to each congressman the number of $100 tickets he had to sell for the Austin political dinner. The congressmen would not have needed those assignments if the governor weren't worried about gathering a full house in Austin. Connally's level of irritation was high. The situation was further complicated by the fact that Senator Yarborough was being given testimonial dinner in Austin only five weeks before the president's. Ticket sales to the Yarborough dinner had been brisk. On top of his worries about conservative donors, he now had to worry whether the liberals would be ready to fork out a second $100 so quickly. Chain-smoking and clearly nervous, Connally now said to the congressmen:

"Listen, boys, the reason *I'm* here is that *I'm* meeting with the president in a few hours about his trip to Dallas. I don't know what to say. They're going to want me to tell them where and when and how to get money in Texas for the party. Now, I've made a few calls around, and frankly, the people who are supporting John Kennedy in Texas are not the ones with money."

At the table was Congressman Henry Gonzalez of San Antonio, whose relationship with John Kennedy went back to the early fifties, when Gonzales had been the only Hispanic on the San Antonio city council, and whose cry "Viva Kennedy!" to an audience in East Harlem during the campaign of 1960 had started a national wave of adulation for Kennedy among Hispanic voters. Gonzalez came to this meeting already in a huff. He had heard that San Antonio was slated to get only a few hours on Kennedy's Texas itinerary, when it was the only major Texas city to go for Kennedy in the 1960 election. Moreover, Gonzalez had promoted the naming of a San Antonio high school after Kennedy, and when it was authorized, it was the only school in America named after the president. The thought of Dallas and Fort Worth getting nearly a full day rankled Gonzalez considerably.

Furthermore, Congressman Gonzalez knew better than anyone at the meeting of the personal dangers that lurked in Texas for national liberals. As the only true New Frontiersman in the Texas delegation, he was the prime recipient of hate mail from the right, and it came to him by the bale. Three months before, he had been one of only twenty congressmen to vote against further funding for the House Un-American Activities Committee, and shortly afterwards, he got a little message from the Minutemen, who among other things, held field exercises with machine guns outside San Antonio.

He took seriously the Minutemen's message: "You are a traitor. We have the hair trigger on your neck." The warning carried a picture of cross hairs in a telescopic sight, and below it, the words, "In Memoriam, Henry B. Gonzalez."

These considerations aside, Gonzalez simply did not like Connally or anything he stood for. During his campaign for governor, Connally had made the mistake of calling up Gonzalez and referring to him in Spanish as *"Papacito Grande,"* the label for the "Big Boss." Gonzalez prided himself on being the man of the people, rather than a big shot who threw his weight around. As he heard Connally poormouth the presidential trip now, his blood boiled.

Connally was saying, "I think [the trip] is a mistake. You know the people who are for Kennedy are the people without money. I've checked with businessmen, and they aren't about to contribute to his campaign—"

"Just a minute, Governor," Gonzalez cut in. "Whom did you call in San Antonio?" Gonzalez knew the answer to his question. If Connally had called anyone in his hometown, it would have been the blue-blood banker, Walter McAllister, or the millionaire builder H.P. "Hap" Zachery, who was a Horatio Alger character like the governor himself. The governor stammered, not about to confess in this crowd.

"—because I know some people in San Antonio who support the president," Gonzalez pressed, and then delivered his shot. "If you called the ones you've been appointing, Governor, they're all Republicans! I'll get you businessmen. You may not like them, though, because they won't support you!" Immediately, an uproar broke out, and the meeting ended in loud, fractious dissension.

When the governor arrived in the Oval Office, President Kennedy greeted him warmly. There was between them a competition of vanities as well as politics, and it was almost sexual. The topic of Connally's good looks had been hotly debated among the Kennedys, and Jack Kennedy had subscribed to Jackie Kennedy's judgment that Connally was "too pretty to be handsome." Now the president pointed to the couch and took his customary place in his rocking chair. The president still had his heart set on four or five fundraisers. Apparently, Lyndon Johnson had made no effort to dissuade him. Connally was prepared.

"Mr. President, I think that is a mistake," he said emphatically. "We want the money, yes, but we also need to position you in such a way that you're going to benefit politically from it, and it doesn't look like all you're interested in is the money of the state. Frankly, if you come down, and we try to get on five fundraising events in the principal cities of Texas, people are going to think that all you're interested in is the financial rape of the state."

That was strong language in 1963, and it registered. The president relented. "Well, alright. What do you suggest?"

Connally laid out his plan, which he said was the product of wide discussion among the Texas political community. He added one final suggestion. He hoped Mrs. Kennedy would come with the president to Texas. All the events would include women, and they would make a fuss about her.

"They want to see what her hairdo looks like and what her clothes look like," Connally said. "It's important to them."

"I agree with you," Kennedy replied. "I'll talk to her about it."

Jackie Kennedy was in Greece, resting on Aristotle Onassis's yacht, trying to get her spirit and her strength back after the tragic death of her child Patrick only two days after he was born.

That evening, Connally went out to the Elms in Northwest Washington to have dinner with the Johnsons, bracing himself. When his meeting with the president was scheduled two weeks before, the White House had specifically requested Connally to keep it confidential from Lyndon Johnson. That had surprised the governor, and he was doubly surprised when Johnson was absent from the Oval Office. At the door, Johnson was visibly irritated.

"I suppose you think I don't have any interest in what happens in Texas?"

"No, Lyndon," Connally replied stiffly. "I know you're extremely interested in what is happening in Texas."

"Why didn't you tell me?" Johnson demanded.

"I assumed you knew I was going to see the president," Connally replied. "After all, it's not my prerogative to say who is in the Oval Office. I assumed if the president wanted you there, you would be there."

Connally was touching a raw nerve, for it was clear enough that Kennedy had not wanted Johnson present. It had been widely noticed that Kennedy acted differently in meetings with Johnson present. The president seemed deferential, even a bit cowed, as if Johnson intimidated him, politically, even physically. Given the bond between Connally and Johnson, Kennedy did not want them to gang up on him.

"You could have told me beforehand what you had in mind," Johnson sulked.

"You knew basically what I had in mind," Connally protested, perhaps too much, thinking of their telephone conversations over the summer. "Anyway, here is what he said…" and he related the substance of the Oval Office conversation. Over the twenty-five years of their intimacy, they had been in this situation many times before. Johnson was hurt by Connally's secretiveness, as if they were not supposed to have any secrets between them; at least, Connally should have none. Connally knew what to do. "I'm sorry, Lyndon," he said softly. "I would have talked to you before I went to see the president. Frankly, I assumed you would be there. When I got into the Oval Office, I was rather surprised that you weren't there, but I had no choice but to go ahead and discuss the trip."

In time, Johnson settled down, as Connally knew he would.

CHAPTER FIVE:

A Suspicious Conversation

That evening, at about the time Governor Connally left the Elms Restaurant in Washington, another social evening in Dallas was drawing to a close. It was the birthday celebration of a Dallas attorney named Carroll Jarnagin, a thirty-seven-year-old plaintiff's lawyer with moderately liberal political views, who had twice unsuccessfully run for the state legislature. Jarnagin was then in the midst of divorce proceedings, stemming from his drinking problem, and he was carousing merrily with a client, a woman he liked to describe as an "exotic dancer" whose stage name was Robin Hood. At various lively clubs in Dallas, Miss Hood could often be seen *en deshabille*, but this was her night off. Toward the end of their social evening – over the course of which Jarnagin had consumed a considerable amount of Johnny Walker Red – Robin Hood proposed that they stop by the Carousel Club. She wanted to talk to the owner, a beefy man named Jack Rubenstein, also known as Jack Ruby, about returning to his stage. When they arrived at the Carousel around 10:00 P.M., Jarnagin was very mellow – he was, in fact, drunk, as he later confessed in a lie-detector test. The couple took a table not far from the ticket booth at the head of the stairs.

Not long after they were settled, Jarnagin observed a wiry man in his twenties at the ticket booth, he would later claim. The individual stood about 5'9" in height, and was oddly dressed for someone out on the town. He was loudly demanding to see Ruby. The bouncer appeared and directed the new arrival to the man whom Robin Hood identified for Jarnagin as the owner. Ruby and his visitor took the table next to them, and the following conversation ensued… according to Carroll Jarnagin.

The transcript of this conversation is contained in number 2821 of the Warren Commission exhibits, but the original remained for decades among the safe-guarded papers of Henry Wade, the Dallas County District Attorney in 1963. (Wade died in 2001.) In February 2008, however, his successor, Craig Watkins, released the document along with other artifacts from Wade's safe such as Oswald's clothing on the day he was murdered and a set of brass knuckles owned by Jack Ruby. In releasing the items, Watkins admitted that he was "always a conspiracy theorist" and "never believed that Lee Harvey Oswald acted alone."

Odd narratives abound in the JFK assassination archives, but Carroll Jarnagin's story – lengthy, detailed, colorful – is one of the oddest. I include it here as an example of how dramatic testimony can generate conspiracy theories, why they are given credence or ultimately debunked, and what type of individual can sometimes be behind them.

According to Jarnagin's transcript, Ruby greeted his caller by name, a name Jarnagin could not recall as he attempted to reconstruct the conversation he said he heard.

"What are you doing here?" Ruby asked.

"Don't call me by my name," the visitor said testily.

"What name are you using?"

"H.L. Lee."

"What do you want?"

"I need some money. I just got in from New Orleans. I need a place to stay, and a job."

"I noticed that you hadn't been around," Ruby said. "What were you doing in New Orleans?"

"There was a street fight, and I got put in jail."

"What charge?"

"Disturbing the peace."

"How did you get back?"

"Hitchhiked. I just got in."

"You have a family, don't you? Can't you stay with them?"

"They're in Irving, and they don't know I'm back. I want to get a place to myself."

"You'll get the money after the job is done."

"What about half now, and half after the job is done?" Lee said.

"No. But don't worry, I'll have the money for you after the job is done."

"How much?" Lee asked.

"We've already agreed on that," Ruby said and then leaned forward to whisper something, which Jarnagin did not hear.

"How do I know that you can do the job?" Ruby asked.

"I'm a Marine sharpshooter."

"Are you sure that you can do the job without hitting anybody but the governor?"

"I'm sure. I've got the equipment ready."

"Have you tested it? Will you need to practice any?"

"Don't worry about that. I don't need any practice. When will the governor be here?"

"Oh, he'll be here plenty of times during campaigns," Ruby replied.

"Where can I do the job?" Lee asked. "From the roof of some building?"

"No, that's too risky. Too many people around."

"But they'll be watching the parade. They won't notice you."

"Afterwards they would tear me to pieces before I could get away."

"Then do it from here – from a window," Ruby said.

"How would I get in?"

"I'll tell the porter to let you in."

"Won't there be people in the place?"

"I can close the place for the parade and leave word with the porter to let you in."

"What about the porter?"

"I can tell him to leave after letting you in. He won't know anything."

"I don't want any witnesses around."

"You'll be alone."

"How do I get away? There won't be much time afterwards."

"The back door."

"What about the rifle? What do I do if the police run in while I'm running out?"

"Hide the rifle. You just heard the shot and ran in from the parade to see what was going on. In the confusion, you can walk out the front door in the crowd."

"No, they might shoot me first," Lee said. "There must be time for me to get out the backway before the police come in. Can you lock the front door after I come in and leave the back door open?"

"That would get me involved. How could I explain that you were in my club with a rifle and the front door locked?"

"You left the front door open, and it was locked from the inside when somebody slipped in, while you were watching the parade. What about the money? When do I get the money?"

"I'll have it here for you."

"But when? I'm not going to have much time after the shooting to get away."

"I'll have the money on me, and I'll run in first and hand it to you and you can run on out the back way."

"I can't wait long. Why can't you leave the money in here?"

"How do I know you'll do the job?"

"How do I know you will show up with the money after the job is done?"

"You can trust me. Besides, you'll have the persuader."

"The rifle? I want to get away from it as soon as it's used."

"You can trust me," Ruby said.

"How about giving me half of the money just before the job is done, and then you can send me the other half later."

"I can't turn the money loose until the job is done. If there's a slip-up and you don't get him, they'll pick the money up immediately. I couldn't tell them I gave half of it to you in advance. They'd think I double-crossed them ... You'll just have to trust me to hand you the money as soon as the job is done. There is no other way ... Remember, they want the job done just as bad as you want the money. After this is done, they may want to use you again."

"Not that it makes any difference, but what have you got against the governor?" Lee asked.

"He won't work with us on paroles. With a few of the right boys out, we could really open up this state, with a little co-operation from the governor. The boys in Chicago have no place to go, no place to operate. They've clamped the lid down in Chicago. Cuba is closed. Everything is dead. Look at this place – half empty. If we can open up this state, we could pack this place every night. Those boys will spend if they have the money. Remember, we're right next to Mexico. There'd be money for everybody, if we can open up this state."

"How do you know that the governor won't work with you?"

"It's no use. He's been in Washington too long. They're too straight up there. After they've been there awhile, they get to thinking like the attorney general. The attorney general ... now there's a guy the boys would like to get, but it's no use. He stays in Washington too much."

"A rifle shoots as far in Washington as it does here, doesn't it?" Lee said.

"Forget it. That would bring the heat on everywhere, and the feds would get into everything. No, forget about the attorney general."

"Killing the governor of Texas will put the heat on too, won't it?"

"Not really, they'll think some crackpot Communist did it, and it will be written off as an unsolved crime."

"That is, if I get away."

"You'll get away. All you have to do is run out the back door."

"What kind of door is there back there? It won't accidentally lock on me, will it?"

"No," Ruby said. "You can get out that way without any trouble. It's a safe way out. I'll show you, but not now."

There was a distraction, and Jarnagin missed some interchanges. Then he heard Lee say, "There's really only one building to do it from, the one that covers main, Elm, and the Commerce."

"Which one is that?" Ruby asked.

"The school book building, close to the triple underpass."

"What's wrong with doing it from here?"

"What if he goes down another street?"

Suddenly, the man called Lee noticed Jarnagin watching him intently. "Who's that?" he said abruptly. "He's from the FBI..." and the conversation terminated. Lee left quickly afterwards.

The following day, October 5, according to Jarnagin, he called the Texas Department of Public Safety and related the conversation. (There is no record of the call.) He requested that the governor be informed, and he felt his report to the authorities had ended his civic duty.

After the assassination, more than a score of witnesses stepped forward with stories of seeing Ruby and Oswald together in conversation before November 22. For the most part, they were cranks and exhibitionists and self-promoters, and they ranged from places across the country as far away as Los Angeles and Denver. But Jarnagin was a professional man, trained in law and in investigation. A judge before whom Jarnagin had practiced law, and who knew him personally, would say that, while eccentric in some of his personal habits – others referred to him as a "lush" – Jarnagin was a credible witness, and that his testimony deserved to be taken seriously. Twenty five years later, appearing on "USA Today on TV" on February 20, 1988, Jarnagin stood by his story and never wavered thereafter.

But the facts belie his certainty. The first news of President Kennedy's intention to come to Dallas appeared in the *Dallas Morning News* on September 26, a week before Governor Connally went to Washington to finalize the plan. On October 3 Oswald returned from his devastating trip to Mexico City, where he had been spurned by both the Cubans and the Russians in an effort to get a visa to Cuba. The following day – the day of the supposed Carousel Club conversation – Oswald is known to have been in Irving, Texas, visiting his wife at the home of her friend, Ruth Paine. (He could, of course, have ended up in Dallas late that evening.) Less than two weeks later, on October 15, Oswald gained his employment at the Texas State Book Depository.

After the assassination Jarnagin would say he recognized Lee Harvey Oswald in the newspaper as the man in Ruby's booth, and he sat down to carefully reconstruct the conversation he supposed he heard seven weeks before, and mailed it special delivery to J. Edgar Hoover at the FBI on December 5, 1963.

Thereafter, Jarnagin was interviewed by over eighteen investigators from various law enforcement agencies. He never altered his story, and he remained a lawyer in good standing with the Texas bar. One of those investigative sessions included a lie-detector test. Among the questions were these:

Did you actually overhear this conversation between Jack Ruby and Lee Harvey Oswald? He answered yes. The indication: False.

Did you actually see Oswald and Ruby at that table on the night of October 4, 1963? He answered yes. The indication: False.

Did you hear this conversation between these two men on that night? Answer: Yes. Indication: False.

Did you deliberately make up this affidavit to get some publicity? Answer: No. Indication: False.

Were you drunk that night? Answer: Yes. Indication: True. In fact, the only true indications in the test dealt with whether he was drinking that night or if he was drunk.

Two months after the assassination, in February 1964, district attorney Henry Wade invited Jarnagin to his home. It should be remembered that Connally and Wade were close friends; they had been at the University of Texas as students together and had roomed together in their naval training. It would have been Wade's duty to prosecute Oswald for murder, but after Oswald's murder, he had to settle for the prosecution of Jack Ruby. The jury had been empanelled, but evidence had not yet been presented, when Jarnagin went to Wade's house. For four hours they talked. Wade found Jarnagin's story startling, but parts of it did not ring true. The suggestion that organized crime was behind the assassination sounded wrong to Wade. If the syndicate was having problems with paroles for mob figures, it would target the district attorney rather than the governor. It was he, not Connally, who would have been on the "firing line" with the mob.

"I can't put you on the stand without being satisfied that you are telling the truth," Wade told Jarnagin. "We've got a good case here; if they prove we are putting an unreliable witness on the stand, it might hurt us."

The conviction of Jack Ruby was Wade's overriding consideration, not the uncovering of a conspiracy. His best evidence, of course, was the television footage of Ruby killing Oswald in the basement of the Dallas police headquarters. It was hard to get more compelling than that. The conspiracy angle only muddied the water for him, and he was disinclined to take seriously the notion that Governor Connally had been Oswald's target. For the country to have lost its president in the greatest crime of the century, when the commander-in-chief might have been an incidental or accidental target, was an irony too grotesque to contemplate.

There are two footnotes to this bizarre tale. Some years later, Henry Wade would tell Dallas journalist Hugh Aynesworth that upon failing the lie detector test, Jarnagin smiled and said, "Some things you remember and others you don't." In addition, included in the trove from Henry Wade's safe in 2008 were district attorney's letters showing that subsequent to the assassination he was working with producers on a Hollywood film, and was considering using the Jarnagin dialogue as part of the script.

"I believe it is important for the film to be factually correct, that it come from official files, that the witnesses who in any way were participants should appear in person in the film, and in my opinion, will result in an excellent film not only of interest at present but the record of events for history," Mr. Wade wrote. The Jarnagin dialogue came from official files.

Jarnagin himself was later to claim that, like so many others who purportedly had information about a conspiracy, he was physically attacked. Shortly after his interview with Henry Wade, he said he was shot in the leg with a drug pellet, laced with amphetamines, which sent him into the hospital for three months. Jarnagin's interpretation of this attack was that there were powerful forces out there that wanted to prevent the testimony that might validate a relationship between Ruby and Oswald or a conspiracy generally.

History has left us with this: The Warren Commission denied there was a conspiracy, denied that Oswald and Ruby ever knew one another, and denied that the Soviets, the Cubans, or organized crime was behind the assault on Connally and Kennedy. Thirteen years later, in 1978, the House Select Committee on Assassinations supported the Warren Commission in denying that the Cubans, the Soviets, or the mob was involved, *but* it berated the Warren Commission for not pursuing more vigorously the conspiracy angle, and indeed concluded that President Kennedy "was probably assassinated as a result of a conspiracy."

It was a conspiracy they were at a loss to describe.

CHAPTER SIX:

Trade-Off

On October 21, a dynamo from Wisconsin named Jerry Bruno, known as the best of the advance men, received official notification of the presidential trip to Texas from Walter Jenkins in Lyndon Johnson's office. Three days later, Bruno got a proposed schedule and was told that it represented Governor Connally's wishes. As a matter of protocol Connally, as the state's governor, was the official host. More importantly, as a matter of purpose, it was Connally's friends – the hostile, the disenchanted, and the annoyed of Texas – to whom the president wanted to appeal. The White House was determined to be accommodating to the governor.

Almost immediately the trouble began. As word of the itinerary got out, the liberals, who were Kennedy's real friends in Texas, howled in protest. San Antonio – the city of "Viva Kennedy!" – would get the president for only a few hours. In Dallas, the governor wanted the president to speak at the shiny, modern Trade Mart, the pride of the Dallas commercial establishment. The president was to be spirited efficiently from one swank event to another, seeing little of the general public.

That was as the liberals saw it. Connally saw it differently. It was his constituency, the moderates and the conservatives, whom the president had specifically expressed an interest in seeing. Connally was accommodating Kennedy and putting himself out considerably to do so, as he devised a set of basically "nonpolitical" events which would give the president a chance to woo his opponents. Among the big businessmen of corporate Texas, Kennedy's actions in rolling back steel prices the previous year remained an open sore. Then the president had employed the FBI, the Justice Department, and the threat of wage-price legislation to browbeat the steel industry into forgoing a major price increase. To the corporate world, this was the worst kind of government interference. In the course of the battle, Kennedy had said the unforgivable about businessmen:

"My father always told me that all businessmen are sons of bitches, but I never believed him until now."

The line reverberated a year later, and Kennedy was still trying to live it down. To Connally, Kennedy had said, "If these business people are silly enough to think I'm going to dismantle the free enterprise system, they're crazy." Connally was content to let Kennedy try to prove he was not the devil. The Trade Mart speech was to be Kennedy's opportunity to do so.

While Connally and his forces pushed to narrow the president's exposure, Yarborough sought to widen it, and the central irony of that tragic trip to Texas lies in the fact that the compromise itself led to a plan that put the president in harm's way. If either Connally or Yarborough had won totally in their demands, the president and the governor would not have been shot. In roads taken and not taken, the fates were cruel.

The man in the middle was Jerry Bruno. Before he left for Texas, Bruno had met with Johnson's man, Walter Jenkins, with the president's appointment secretary, Ken O'Donnell, in the White House, and with Yarborough's lieutenant. They briefed the advance man on the feud between the Texas Guelphs and Ghibellines. It all sounded pretty routine to Bruno, who always encountered factions when he advanced political trips. This did not worry him. His experience told him that political competition is always put aside in deference to what is best for the president and the nation. Of Connally, O'Donnell had made only one off-the-cuff remark. "You're dealing with an arrogant guy here," he said, but that was hardly novel either. Bruno arrived in Austin on October 28, scheduled to go to lunch with the governor at the Four Acres the next day.

In their private dinner room, only a few bites into the appetizer, Connally made it manifestly clear that he *and only he* was going to run this show. He presented Bruno with the president's itinerary as a *fait accompli*. "It's going to be my way or no way," Connally announced. "This is it, or he can stay home."

Bruno wasn't prepared for quite this level of high-handedness, and he grew more unsettled as he looked over the schedule Connally gave him. It was not well worked out.

"Well, I want to look over all the sites," Bruno said. "I'll make a report to the White House, and they'll get back to you."

Customary as this procedure was, it unhinged Connally. Leaping out of his chair, the governor strode to a telephone in the corner of the room, picked it up and in a loud voice demanded to be connected with the White House. When Ken O'Donnell came on the line, Connally went over the itinerary with him in a loud stage voice for Bruno's benefit. After four or five minutes on the phone, Connally hung up and returned to the table.

"It's all confirmed," he said. "This is the itinerary." Bruno wondered why he had come. (In fact, O'Donnell had not confirmed the Connally schedule at all.)

The following day the advance man toured the proposed sites with Cliff Carter, an aide to Lyndon Johnson. At each site he was greeted by a Connally man and a Yarborough man. As the opposing forces tugged in opposite directions, confusion was the result.

San Antonio, Houston, and Austin looked fine to Bruno, but Dallas and Fort Worth were problems. Three decisions had to be made. Had they been made differently, they would have changed the course of history. One represented a victory for Connally, one a victory for Yarborough, and the third was a loss for both. They are the three Furies of Dallas.

The first had to do with the possibility of an honorary degree being conferred on Kennedy at Texas Christian University in Fort Worth. Connally had broached the idea to the TCU president and he had liked it. It provided a dignified event for Connally's hometown, and it became the raison d'être for the Fort Worth stop. Connally had promised the honor to Kennedy at the White House, and Kennedy was pleased, since the conferring of a degree by a bedrock Protestant university would further bury the fears of the South over a Catholic president. To Bruno at lunch, the event was presented as a done deal. As a scheduling matter, this would work well. The degree ceremony was to be in the midmorning and then the presidential caravan would motor the thirty miles to Dallas for the president's speech to Dallas businessmen. It was unlikely, under this plan, that there would be time for a motorcade through downtown Dallas, but if there were, it would follow a fairly direct course.

As the planning went forward, Bruno got a call from Connally. He was sorry, but TCU had decided against conferring the degree. The refusal had been presented to Connally as a matter of university regulations and traditions. To follow the normal process, the faculty senate and the student senate would have to approve the degree, and there was not enough time for such deliberations. The elders and the sticklers within the university administration were concerned that a bad precedent might be set if rules were skirted just for the president of the United States. It might politicize degree granting in the future. Bruno did not buy it. In the first place, Connally had said the logistics were set; the degree had been promised to the president a month before; Connally was supposed to be in total control. What was the real reason?

"Well, he's a Catholic, you know," Connally told Bruno.

What were they to do? There was no reason to go to Fort Worth now. "Let me straighten this thing out," Connally said. "I'll give it some thought." Sometime later the governor called back and announced that the Fort Worth Chamber of Commerce would like to give the president a breakfast. One could always count on the local chamber of commerce to pinch hit in the event of a snafu. Bruno's annoyance was rising.

For all Connally's puffing about how he *and only he* was in control, how he *and only he* could make a success of the presidential visit, he had thrown things into chaos. Instead of a leisurely sleepover in Houston after a testimonial dinner for Congressman Albert Thomas, the president would now have to fly to Fort Worth near midnight so he could be ready for the hastily pasted-up breakfast. More important, there were now two hours in the late morning that needed to be filled. To kill time, rather than save it, it was decided that Kennedy would *fly* from Fort Worth to Dallas. All the motion to and from airports would consume the dead space in the schedule. From the Dallas airport to the luncheon speech, the motorcade route was redrawn and lengthened, taking it through Dealey Plaza.

The second Fury watched over the motorcade itself. Connally opposed it vigorously. Having bent the itinerary out of shape, he was now worried that too much was being packed into the president's schedule. Lyndon Johnson's campaigns of 1941 and 1948 came to his mind, and he knew that by overloading schedules you could "work a man to death." If he did not want to advance the cause of Kennedy liberalism in Texas, neither did he want the president to flop. Kennedy should be rested. He should look good, his voice should be strong, and he should exude enthusiasm. A motorcade, Connally knew, was hard work.

"It's very tiring. It's exhausting," he argued. "You assume

that a person is just riding along, so there shouldn't be any difficulty. But in a motorcade the president is trying even in a fleeting second to make contact with thousands and tens of thousands of people along a parade route. He's looking from one side to another. Even if he catches a human eye for one second, there is a communication. I'm telling you, it's a strain."

The governor also feared an embarrassment in Dallas, and a motorcade was an invitation. Connally's negotiator with the White House, Frank Erwin, a corporate lawyer and Democratic committeeman, voiced more specific fears that the supporters of General Edwin Walker would find this a prime opportunity.

To the liberals and to the White House, the elitist quality of the Connally plan was unconscionable. If the president was intent on speaking to Connally's exclusive businessmen's lunch, his exposure to Yarborough's people must be in the streets. Moreover, Kennedy himself was sentimental about the technique of the open motorcade. He attributed part of his success against Richard Nixon in 1960 to his mingling with the people by means of a motorcade. On this point, the liberals won.

The last Fury presided over the decision about the site for Kennedy's luncheon speech in Dallas. As mentioned, Connally had specified the Trade Mart, a boxy commercial complex just off Stemmons Freeway, where the hall for the luncheon was about the right size for the audience Connally was putting together and which, he thought, had the pizzazz of the Kennedys themselves. The Dallas establishment was rightly proud of the building, for it projected the kind of energetic image modern Dallas strove for. The alternative was the Women's Building – a venerable, if mundane, mainstay for larger downtown functions, located near the Cotton Bowl at the State Fairgrounds, and not far from Big Tex (the symbol of the Texas ethos, who stands 52 feet tall, wears size 70 boots, and sports a 75-gallon hat). The Secret Service and the White House preferred it. The Women's Building had a larger banquet hall large enough to accommodate a Jacksonian feast for over 4,000, and this was more in the Kennedy and Yarborough populist style. Moreover, the banquet hall at the fairgrounds undercut one of Connally's most embarrassing propositions: that at each presidential meal there should be a three-tiered head table, where Connally would sit with the president at the highest tier, and Yarborough would occupy a lower station with lesser personages. To Bruno, and to everyone, the thrust of this was obvious.

"John Connally wanted to show that Ralph Yarborough had no support from the president," Bruno has said. "This was to be demonstrated in front of the public, in front of the big contributors, and it would be done with the president at Connally's side. The point was to downgrade Yarborough and to humiliate him publicly." But the hall at the Women's Building had too low a ceiling for these classes of importance.

The Secret Service liked the Women's Building for other reasons. If the event were held there, the route of the motorcade would be more direct, continuing straight down Main Street, picking up speed as it entered Dealey Plaza and zipping through the small park at forty to fifty miles an hour. If the Trade Mart were the spot, the motorcade would have to slow nearly to a stop to make a right turn onto Houston Street, and then a left turn at the next street, Elm. It was the deceleration to a crawling speed that concerned the Secret Service, especially since the route of the motorcade was to be published, and any nut could quickly determine where he might get the best shot at the president.

The Texas State Book Depository on Dealey Plaza had no particular significance for the authorities before the assassination, but it should have, since the Dallas FBI had a file on the Oswalds. Initially, its interest was in Marina Oswald in a routine case of keeping track of a Russian émigré, although Lee Harvey Oswald was also in the file as a subscriber to the Communist newspaper, *The Daily Worker*. But the case became more active in August 1963 when the New Orleans FBI office reported that Lee Oswald had gotten in a street scuffle as he distributed Communist leaflets there with a placard around his neck reading "Hands off Cuba, Viva Fidel." And it became even more active when in late October 1963, the agent in charge of the case, James Hosty, received a dispatch reporting that Oswald had made a contact with the Soviet Embassy in Mexico City. Still, Hosty was working between 25 and 40 cases at any given time, and tracking Oswald had no special urgency. On November 1, three weeks before the assassination, the agent finally found Marina Oswald, living separately in the Dallas suburb of Irving, Texas, with her child and new baby. Facing an FBI agent looking for her husband, Marina Oswald went berserk as visions of Soviet secret police passed through her mind. Agent Hosty decided not press a frightened witness, and he backed off.

Three days later, on November 4, Hosty learned that Oswald was working at the Texas Book Depository in Dallas and called the personnel office there to confirm Oswald's employment there. But that was the end of it. He did not pass Oswald's name to the Secret Service, even when he learned on November 19 that the presidential motorcade would pass slowly through Dealey Plaza.

Lee Harvey Oswald did not get Hosty's attention again until November 22. The agent watched the presidential motorcade mosey through downtown Dallas, and then went to lunch. A day later, he was interviewing Oswald in the Dallas police station. When the agent entered the room, Oswald was ranting about the Gestapo and the secret police. When the FBI agent was introduced, Oswald shouted at him:

"Oh, so you're Hosty. I've heard about you. If you want to talk to me, don't bother my wife. Come see me!"

Later, the Bureau would say that it had no reason to consider Oswald a dangerous security threat, but the assassination led to considerable soul-searching within law enforcement circles about the general psychological profile for potential presidential assassins.

*   *   *   *   *

The Secret Service had other reservations about the Trade Mart. A series of low-slung catwalks loomed above the lobby through which the president would walk. Bruno took photographs of them, for he was concerned that it might not be possible to secure them totally. When Bruno showed the photographs to the head of the White House detail of the Secret

Service, he said,

"We'll *never* go there."

On this issue Connally dug in his heels. His mouthpiece, Frank Erwin, warned the White House that if the businessmen Connally had so ticklishly inveigled into attending the lunch had to mix with Yarborough liberals and labor leaders and ethnics, they would boycott. Erwin kept mentioning the "nonpolitical flavor" of the event, as if Connally's choice of an audience wasn't itself political.

Only days before the president's arrival, the struggle over the hall in Dallas had become ugly, so ugly that Connally was threatening to cancel the entire trip. In the minds of the Kennedy people, the main purpose of the trip was to civilize the two factions within the Texas Democratic party, so that Kennedy could have a reasonably united party behind his campaign in 1964. No one on the White House team accepted Connally's notion that greed for Texas political money compelled the trip. In the opinion of Larry O'Brien, the president's chief political strategist, the trip would not have been undertaken at all except for the testimonial dinner for the powerful Congressman Albert Thomas of Houston. Kenneth O'Donnell's attitude was that there was not much the White House was going to get out of the trip. But Texas was a big and important state; the president had to go there, and they should all try to make the best of it. What was proposed for fund raising in Texas was no different from arrangements already undertaken or contemplated in a number of other presidential trips, as the Democratic Party began to gear up for the national election.

In fact, Connally wanted major political rewards for his efforts on behalf of the president. He wanted Kennedy to quash the serious liberal opposition that was developing a challenge to his reelection as governor. As it was shaping up, his prospective opponent was Don Yarborough, who was related to Senator Ralph Yarborough only in a political sense. To Bruno, during the planning for the presidential trip, Connally said more than once, "When is Ken O'Donnell or Larry O'Brien going to get Don Yarborough off my back?" Through this descent toward disaster, Jerry Bruno kept a chronicle in his diary.

October 28: Talked with Senator Yarborough. The Senator is bitter because he's afraid that Connally would run the show with Lyndon Johnson and he doesn't trust the two of them. Yarborough said, "They never liked Jack Kennedy – they never have, and they never will. I'll give you a man in each city to help you with the details."… It's obvious from talking that the problem surrounding the whole trip revolves around Don Yarborough, who indicated he would run against Governor Connally in the gubernatorial primary. Connally wants President Kennedy to stop Yarborough by using his influence.

October 29: Met with Hank Brown, president of AFL-CIO, a liberal and a friend of Senator Yarborough … He warned me that Connally would try to run the show and keep labor from participating.

October 30: (Dallas) I objected to the Trade Mart because it has four catwalks that span across (the ceiling of) the hall where it would be easy for someone to insult the President and where it would be difficult to get him off without creating a scene.

November 5: I began to find out why Governor Connally is so violently opposed to the Fair Grounds. His intention is to have

two head tables, on two tiers, one which would seat the Presi-
dent, himself, the Vice President, and the head of the (Dallas) Cit-
izens Council. The other would seat a congressional delegation and
would purposely eliminate Yarborough. The Fair Grounds has a
low ceiling that would not accommodate Connally's plan. Con-
nally continues to insist that if the President will not speak at the
Trade Mart, he would not come to Dallas.

November 14: The feud has become so bitter that I went to the
White House to ask Bill Moyers, deputy director of the Peace Corps,
and close to both Connally and Johnson, to try to settle the dis-
pute for the good of the President and the Party. On this day, Ken
O'Donnell decided that there was no way but to go to the Mart.

Bruno was appalled at Connally's warrior attitude. The
governor's pose, he felt, was akin to a European baron riding
through the peasant fields. Bruno waited in vain for the interests of the president to transcend the local feuding. "With
John Connally, it was always what was best for Dallas and
Texas," Bruno would say later with some bitterness. "If I heard
the phrase 'Dallas business community' once, I heard it a thousand times. His concern was big money. He operated solely on
raw power. He was intent to put people in their place." Bruno
was becoming so upset at Connally's power play that he was
losing his effectiveness. Bill Moyers, former special assistant
to President Johnson, moved into the situation, feeling that he
could smooth things over, but he soon found out differently.
From Texas, he called Bruno in Washington to consult, and
they began to snipe at one another over the implacability of
Connally.

"Your nose is out of joint because I'm here, and you're not,"

Moyers charged.

"Connally is not concerned one whit for the president or the country," Bruno fired back. "He's a selfish, greedy, arrogant bastard." Moyers hung up on him.

On November 15, Bruno made his final entry in his diary: *"The White House announced that the Trade Mart had been approved. I met with O'Donnell and Moyers who said that Connally was unbearable and on the verge of cancelling the trip. They decided they had to let the Governor have his way."*

In the decision over the Trade Mart, Connally had won.

CHAPTER SEVEN:

November 21, 1963

Aboard Air Force One, the avuncular Congressman Henry Gonzalez settled in beside Olin "Tiger" Teague, the powerful House leader from Central Texas, a veteran of the Normandy invasion who had been elected the year after the war ended and was the most decorated soldier in Congress. There was a lot for these senior and junior Democratic members of the House to worry about. The glow of the Test Ban Treaty did not blind anyone to the fact that the president's basic relationship with Congress had broken down: for the first time in history not one appropriation bill had been passed through the current session. The administration's problems with so basic a matter as appropriations provided one more justification for the president to come personally to a dinner honoring Albert Thomas, for the Houstonian was a senior member of the House Appropriations Committee.

But appropriations weren't the only problem. Kennedy's civil rights program, the centerpiece of his domestic policy, was stalled, and this failure had ensnared other objectives like an elementary education bill, his Medicare proposal, and wide-ranging measures in conservation. To many Texans, Kennedy was all flash and no substance. His own poll showed that only thirty-eight percent of Texas approved of what he was doing as president. If a Kennedy-Johnson ticket was to have any chance whatever against Barry Goldwater in 1964, the state party machinery would have to be strong and unified, and the governor would need to put all the power at his command behind the national ticket.

These were the wider legislative and political concerns, but Gonzalez was now preoccupied with more immediate annoyances. He was still angry over the brevity of Kennedy's stay in San Antonio, and about the spurning of his pet project, the John F. Kennedy High School, which was only a few blocks from Kelly Air Force Base, where the president was scheduled to depart San Antonio. How many John F. Kennedy High Schools were there in Boston? Gonzalez had asked Robert Kennedy only a few days earlier. Gonzalez also hoped for an occasion on this trip to needle the president again about his Vietnam policy. He had been doing so on and off for six months. The Air Force had decorated his godson, a helicopter cargo master, for over 300 combat missions in Vietnam when the official national policy proclaimed America's role to be solely advisory. The godson, who Gonzalez called simply Miguel, Jr., had been one of fifty-seven American advisers in Vietnam. Miguel, Jr. had requested his godfather to secure a .45 pistol for him the day after he had been exposed to hostile fire during a drop over Vietcong territory, when he had to grab the rifle of his ARVN counterpart to open fire in the jungle. How could the president put boys like his Miguel on the firing line and not give them the means to defend themselves?

"What do you think is going to happen in Dallas?" Teague said, breaking Gonzalez's reverie.

Tiger Teague was scarcely the type to tremble delicately over nothing, but he too worried about Dallas. Several nights before in Washington, the editor of the *Dallas Times Herald*, Felix McKnight, had spent the night at Teague's house and had engendered real anxiety in Teague about the safety of the president in Dallas.

"Some embarrassment – that's about all," Gonzalez said distantly. He remembered a function for Wilbur Mills only a few weeks before, when Kennedy had been heckled and had made his hecklers look ridiculous.

"Jack be nimble, Jack be quick," he said now.

At that moment, the president emerged from his forward compartment, smoking a small, thin cigar, looking pinkishly healthy. In the soft light of the plane, Gonzalez took note again of the startling blueness of the president's eyes. He would never forget them. Jokes about the cigar, whether it was Cuban and all of that, were passed around – Gonzalez had never before seen Kennedy smoke – and there were jokes about a Raymond Moley column in the current issue of *Newsweek*, in which the conservative columnist urged Barry Goldwater to hold fast to his hard starboard course so that he could offer a clear alternative to Kennedy and what his administration "is giving us now."

"I saw that," Kennedy said. "I don't think Barry is going to have time for a presidential campaign, though. He's too busy dismantling the federal government."

He might make light of Goldwater, but Kennedy knew he was headed for a state that was likely to prefer Goldwater to him, and he knew that a *Houston Chronicle* poll due out shortly would indicate the extent of the deficit. But he had no deficit in San Antonio, and Gonzalez, one more time, complained about the shortness of his stay there, the only terra firma for Kennedy.

"Yes, yes, Henry," Kennedy said good-naturedly. "You've told me those winning numbers in Bexar County ad nauseam. I've given your area a veteran's hospital. We've made it into a postal distribution center. As I remember, I gave you an hour's lead time on those announcements, so you got pretty good credit there."

Gonzalez was not to be put off, and he pressed until he got a promise. "Okay, Henry, next year, February or March," Kennedy said finally. "I'll come back to San Antonio and stay as long as you want. First, I've got to go to CINCPAC in Honolulu and review the whole Southeast Asia business." The president started back to his compartment. Then, at the door, he turned back to Gonzalez. In the years to come, Gonzalez would keep this fleeting moment frozen in his mind, as his last direct personal touch with the deified president, but also as a fulcrum of history.

"Oh, and by the way, Henry, I've already ordered all the men and all the helicopters to be out of South Vietnam by the end of the year." And he was gone.

Farther back in the plane, the wily, prickly, and altogether suspicious Senator Yarborough was pondering how to make his way through the minefield of the next few days. Connally's strategy to humiliate him – no doubt in cahoots with Johnson – was apparent enough by this time. It was to come at the main political event of the trip, the extravaganza in Austin, when "the long knives of Austin," as they were later dubbed, were to be drawn. If the senior senator from Texas was to be introduced at all, it would be among an anonymous pack of state legislators. Preceding the political dinner, there was to be a reception at the Governor's Mansion, and Yarborough had been ostentatiously left off the list of the invited. While this was a political decision by Connally, Nellie Connally had personalized it. She would not have "that man" in her house.

Yarborough stewed. He was a veteran of these personal slights. On the June 5 trip to El Paso with President Kennedy, Yarborough had started up the aisle after the president, when he found his way physically barred until Kennedy was down the ramp and across the tarmac past the line of photographers. Then, in the motorcade going into town, Yarborough listened impatiently as Kennedy asked Connally about his state's woeful standing in education and public health. (Texas was then 38th in the nation in education and 36th in public health.)

Senator Yarborough was not a devious man by nature. He cared about protocol, and yet it seemed to him that his scramble for respect, despite his unfailing support of the Kennedy program, would never end. He had to fight for his dignity every step of the way. As for the reception at the Governor's Mansion, Yarborough had a Jacksonian view of such occasions: any function with the president made it a presidential party, and the president rather than a mere governor should have an influence over who was invited. Still, his best course now, Yarborough thought, was to keep quiet and let things ride. For months his standing in the polls had been five to ten percentage points ahead of Kennedy's in Texas, and well ahead of Connally's. There were persistent rumors that Lyndon Johnson would be dropped from the ticket in 1964. As Air Force One winged toward Texas, Richard Nixon was telling an audience that Lyndon Johnson was a liability to the Democrats and would be dropped.

Yarborough's determination to keep quiet was ruled by his brain, but on the plane when a pool reporter approached him about the intended discourtesy in Austin, his emotions took over.

"I've had many telephone calls and letters from friends because Mrs. Yarborough and I were not invited to the mansion…," he began casually.

The reporter pressed harder. "How does it feel to be slapped in the face?"

"Well, I'm not surprised. Governor Connally is so terribly uneducated governmentally. How could you expect anything else?"

In Houston, meanwhile, Connally had gone on too long in a speech to the Texas Manufacturers Association in the Sheraton-Lincoln Hotel and had frantically prevailed upon a friendly oilman to lend him a jet to pop over to San Antonio. With Air Force One already in its final approach, Connally's plane slipped into the pattern just ahead of it, and a relieved governor rushed over to pump a few hands and take his place next to Nellie in the receiving line.

The reception in San Antonio was warm, even tumultuous. With her fragile beauty, Jackie Kennedy was the instant star, as Connally had predicted. The throngs clamored for a glimpse and a shy wave. Taking her first bunch of yellow roses, she glided ethereally alongside her husband through the receiving line, as across the tarmac the crowd beckoned at the chain-link fence. Here, there was no nastiness. Only one placard dotted the crowd:

JOHN CONNALLY!
WHY ARE YOU AGAINST EQUAL RIGHTS?
EQUAL URBAN REPRESENTATION?

From a distance, Henry Gonzalez watched as Kennedy strode to the fence to work the crowd. To his companion he said, in the first of the premonitions, how easy it would be – *how easy.* Someone had once put a .38 to his stomach and pulled the trigger, and though the gun didn't go off, every time he went into a boisterous crowd in the barrios of San Antonio and the cascarones, eggs filled with confetti were lobbed his way, he was apprehensive. Inevitably, he ducked as if his car were a foxhole. And he remembered the sourness of Wilbur Mills a few days before, when the old congressman had turned to him and snarled, "That damn princeling, silver spoon in his mouth, what the hell does he know about Texas?" How easy it would be.

To the national press, another royal visit of the Kennedys to the outlying provinces was no story at all. They sensed that one purpose of this trip was to heal a political rift, and they smelled an old fashioned cockfight. Yarborough's comment on the plane had swept through the entire entourage, and now they watched hungrily as the motorcade formed, knowing that the senator was supposed to ride with the vice president. If Connally had been warned never to give Yarborough an inch, Yarborough's friends were telling him not to buckle under to the Connally-Johnson plot to humiliate him.

The senator had not understood that he was supposed to ride with Johnson anyway. Larry O'Brien had promised him that he could ride with the most popular local figures at each stop – Albert Thomas in Houston, Henry Gonzalez in San Antonio – and that was fine with him. Now, a Secret Service man, Rufus Youngblood, directed him to the vice president's car. It was a glitch in the White House planning, for Youngblood was acting on Kenneth O'Donnell's orders. Yarborough puffed up in indignation. Here was an ex-colonel in the army being ordered around by a sergeant. He would not have it. He freelanced.

"Henry, can I hitch a ride with you?" he asked, finding Gonzalez near at hand, and he clambered in with the congressman. For a moment there was confusion, a moment long enough for the press gleefully to notice a motorcade with each car packed, except for the vice president's where a glum Johnson sat alone with his lady. The vice president was losing face; and the press at last had something to write about.

The wind was high, gusting to thirty-five miles an hour, as the motorcade took off. For the first time the Connallys sensed Jackie Kennedy's discomfort and ill ease. She was worried about her hair, as was Nellie about hers, but Nellie was accustomed to wind in her hair. If only the bubbletop were affixed – but the president had resisted. It put more distance between him and the people, making him feel like a laboratory experiment. Now, Jackie asked to swap seats with the governor so she could get more protection from the car's windscreen, and so before the sparse crowds on the outskirts of town, the governor and the First Lady clambered over one another. The president did not like that, just as he would not like it in Dallas the next day when Jackie put on her sunglasses. The crowds wanted to see her as much as her husband; Connally had told him so. So he insisted that the governor get back into the jump seat, and she get back into the back seat beside him – "where you belong." Nellie would later repeat the quip affectionately when later she recounted the day.

Before a crowd of ten thousand at the new School of Aerospace Medicine – only a month before the first Saturn rocket would be launched in the program that would eventually realize Kennedy's goal of an American on the moon before the end of the decade – the president invoked one of his patented touches. He borrowed an image from the Irish writer Frank O'Connor about boys making their way across the countryside, and "when they came to an orchard wall that seemed too high to climb, too doubtful to try, too difficult to permit their journey to continue, they took off their caps and tossed them over the wall, and then they had no choice but to follow them." So it was with the American space program.

This trip was to become a contrast of styles. The day before in Dallas, speaking to a convention of soda pop distributors, Johnson had done his earnest best to promote the administration's accomplishments in defense and with the economy, where corporate profits were up thirty percent. There were still gaps, said Johnson, like four million unemployed. That reminded him of the hillbilly who said about the holes in his roof, "When it shines, they don't leak. When it rains, I can't get on the roof to fix them."

The governor, however, would have reason to be pleased with the president's first day in Texas. San Antonio went well, with larger crowds along the motorcade route than he expected. But that was Kennedy country. Dallas would right the balance. Then they had hopped over to Houston, and there, too, the crowds were large, if somewhat more subdued. Connally was also relishing his torment of Yarborough. Albert Thomas had come to the governor as the first peacemaker, specifically at the request of the president, and asked Connally to back off. Why not have Yarborough introduce the vice president at his testimonial dinner that night, before Connally introduced the president? Connally thought that was a lousy idea, and Thomas dropped it. He still had a few points to score. It remained an open question whether Yarborough would be seated at the head table the next night in Austin, for Connally was still hoping for his three tiers. The warfare was psychological now, and Connally wanted Yarborough in a state of animated suspense a while longer.

At the Rice Hotel in Houston, Connally and Yarborough were, embarrassingly, put on the same floor, as they got ready for the Albert Thomas dinner. Guards were posted warily at each door, lest the men emerge by accident at the same time and have to ride down on the same elevator.

At the dinner attended by the "backbone of Houston," the signs were good. The industrialists and the oilmen listened attentively to the president. The Kennedy glamour captured them, and they applauded enthusiastically. Connally too admired the Kennedy wit and style that night. The president's short speech was "burnished with clever touches," he thought, as when Kennedy praised Thomas as the great champion of the space program and referred to the Saturn rocket as "firing the largest payroll – I mean payload – into space," or when the president talked of old men with their dreams and young men with their visions, Thomas being old enough and young enough to have both. In Kennedy, Connally saw himself. When people said he brought the same effortless grace and wit to public life in Texas, he was flattered.

There had been one snafu toward the end of the evening. At the conclusion of the dinner, the crush had separated the president and the governor, and before Connally knew it, Kennedy had left for the airport without him. Connally was frantic, for he did not want to cause the delay of Air Force One, taking off with a crowd of well-fed but tired and easily irritated politicians. Luckily, he managed to commandeer a squad car, and a wild ride through downtown Houston ensued – lights flashing and sirens blasting, going the wrong way up one-way streets, over curbs, through driveways, bumping through gas stations, until the policeman at the wheel finally found the Gulf Freeway and reached speeds close to one hundred miles an hour. Connally loved it.

Finally, after the presidential party had settled for the night in the Texas Hotel in Fort Worth, Connally repaired to the cafeteria for eggs and bacon and milk. This was his hour of the day. An aide gossiped excitedly about the Johnson-Yarborough tiff. "I don't care who rides in which car," Connally said merrily, for, of course, there was no doubt about his own seating arrangements. Upstairs, the Kennedys were settling into their suite, which he and Nellie had decorated for them, appointed with Van Goghs and Monets borrowed from Connally's art-loving friends in town. He knew it would be appreciated – and it was, eventually. It underscored both the Kennedyesque classiness of the Connallys and the classiness of the Texas upper crust.

His opponents had good reason to be buoyed as well. Before the Thomas gala the Kennedys had had dinner alone with the publisher of the *Houston Chronicle*. In deference to the president's visit, the paper delayed the publication of a political poll until Kennedy left town. From the publisher, the president got the news in advance. Goldwater would defeat him in Texas by four percentage points, 52%-48%. Connally was running somewhat stronger, looking like a comfortable winner over any potential challenger. But Senator Yarborough was well ahead of them all in Texas. The senator had been waiting for his local popularity to register with the president, so it would wash away that tripe that he was sure Connally and Johnson were promoting – that hogwash about him being a drag on the Democratic ticket. On the short ride between Houston and Fort Worth that night, Kennedy remarked to Yarborough in a tone markedly more warm and inviting then the day before, "Ralph, you're doing very well in Texas, I hear."

In fact, in his private conversations, Kennedy was actively

rallying to Yarborough's defense. If there was anything that could be done about the rift between the two factions of the Texas Democratic party, only Lyndon Johnson could accomplish it, for only he bridged the gulf between the two camps. The vice president had associated himself ardently with the progressive thrust of the Kennedy program, and he was Connally's closest friend. That night, in the Rice Hotel, Kennedy and Johnson had their last private chat. It was stormy. Kennedy criticized the treatment of Yarborough, childish and undignified as it clearly was. While only the two men were present and no record exists of what they said, the result was that Johnson marched fuming from Kennedy's suite.

To criticize the treatment of Yarborough put Johnson between two competing loyalties. Connally was running the show, and it is likely that the president turned his Yankee scalpel on the governor in front of Johnson. Then he probably demanded to know why Johnson was so powerless to get the sides together. Did he not realize the importance of unity to their own reelection? The reason for Johnson's powerlessness, of course, was personal rather than political. Only a few months before, Yarborough had publicly called Johnson a "power-mad Texas politician" after the senator seized the notion that Johnson had blocked his appointment to the Senate Appropriations Committee. Johnson had cut off many politicians for saying milder things than this in public. Too many outrages and atrocities had passed between the men over the years. Their antipathy, as Connally put it, was implacable.

As Johnson stormed out of Kennedy's suite, Jackie came from the bedroom to wonder about the fuss. She would later tell William Manchester what had been said.

"He sounded mad," she observed, as she watched Johnson's coattails disappear.

"That's just Lyndon. He's in trouble."

Suddenly, apparently from nowhere, Jackie blurted out her distaste for John Connally. There was something about him that she viscerally disliked. "I can't stand being around him all day," she said. "He is just one of those men – oh, I don't know. I just can't bear him sitting there saying all those great things about himself. And he seems to be needling you all day."

"You mustn't say you dislike him, Jackie," the president replied. "If you say it, you'll begin thinking it, and it will prejudice how you act toward him."

But she did think it, and she wasn't the first woman to feel that way. Many other women had taken a similar instinctive dislike to Connally. His arrogance repelled them, making them feel demeaned in his presence. It was all too apparent that they were ornaments to him, there to decorate the room and comfort the men in it. Few accomplished women were ever swept away by him.

In her oral history for the LBJ Library, Jackie Kennedy was to describe her husband's attitude toward Connally on that last night in Houston. "I know he was annoyed with him then. I remember asking that night in Houston what the trouble was. He said that John Connally wanted to show that he was independent and could run on his own. He was making friends with a lot of 'Republican fat cats,' and he wanted to show that he didn't need Lyndon Johnson. Part of the trouble of the trip was [Connally] trying to show that he had his own constituency."

CHAPTER EIGHT:

November 22, 1963

O ver the past five decades, much has been learned about President Kennedy's fragile health, a history that he went to great lengths to cover up: his adrenal insufficiency known as Addison's Disease, his knee pain from an old football injury at Harvard, his neck stiffness, his severe allergies to horses and dogs and house dust, his thyroid insufficiency and anemia, even his defect from birth that made his whole left side appreciably lower than his right, a disparity that aggravated the stress on his lower back, manifested as chronic sacroiliac joint strain.

His back problems began with the explosion of his PT 109 boat in the Pacific Ocean in 1944, and the extreme exertion of swimming a great distance to safety, dragging injured crewmates with him. That led to his first back operation to address a ruptured intervertebral disc. But the pain did not go away. Chronically, well into his presidency, he suffered from terrible back spasms. His second operation, in the mid-1950s was a lumbar fusion procedure where a metal plate was inserted in his lower back. But the operation was botched, making his pain even worse and leading to an infection. A third operation was required to remove the metal plate, and that left him with, by his own description, a "sickly gaping hole" in his back. In 1955 when he first consulted with Dr. Janet Travell (later his personal physician in the White House), he could scarcely walk and had great difficulty in navigating several steps to her New York office.

When he was hospitalized for these various conditions, especially in the 1950s, as he was nurturing presidential ambitions, he and his doctor went to elaborate lengths to keep his hospitalizations secret, even to the extent of posting assumed names on his hospital doors and hiding his medical chart at the nursing station. Once he was president, his medical records were stored in a vault next to the desk of his personal secretary, Evelyn Lincoln. Only after his death did the details of the extraordinary panoply of injections, stimulants, and medications come to light: cortisone shots, codeine painkillers, barbiturates, stimulants like Ritalin, amphetamines, and gamma globulin injections. During his worst periods Dr. Travell was injecting him with procaine shots two or three times a day. But for public consumption, the PT 109 and his rocking chair served as the heroic and poignant symbols of the president's physical difficulties.

To alleviate the pain and to promote an image of a youthful, vigorous leader, Dr. Travell had prescribed an elaborate back brace. Members of Kennedy's inner circle had often witnessed the painful ritual that Kennedy endured in his private

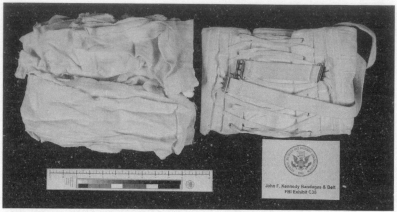

JFK's back brace and ace bandage.

quarters before he ventured in public, when his valet, George Thomas, would literally winch the canvas corset around the president's torso. Metal stays anchored the brace, and a stiff plastic pad covered the area of his sacrum. The valet would yank on the heavy straps and tighten the shoe-lace-like thongs loop by loop in a scene reminiscent of Mamie winching Scarlett O'Hara into her corset in *Gone with the Wind*. After the corset reached maximum tightness, a six-inch wide, elasticized Ace bandage was wrapped in a figure-eight between the president's legs and then wrapped over the corset around his waist to tighten it further and keep it from slipping.

Once in it, the president was veritably planted upright, trapped, immobilized, and almost mummified into a ramrod posture. Many would wonder how JFK could even move in such a contraption. Yet, move he did, and besides his painkillers, his corset contributed to the youthful, high-shouldered military bearing that he presented to the world.

Early on the morning of November 22, the ritual took

place as usual.

* * * * *

As the morning of November 22 broke, Jackie Kennedy remained the object of fascination to the outside world. As the Texas papers gleefully reported the distasteful bickering of various Texas politicians, her star power transcended it all. The other women, Lady Bird and Nellie, fretted about what to wear when they were seen with Jackie. As the Connallys dressed and looked out the window at the workmen across the street, they chatted amiably about how Jackie seemed to loosen up as the day's campaigning wore on, and by nightfall actually seemed to be enjoying herself. They agreed she would be indispensable in the forthcoming campaign.

Six stories below, on the eighth floor, the president had an early meeting with Lawrence O'Brien. Before them lay the early edition of the *Dallas Morning News*, ablaze with gossip about snubs, slights, and insults among the supporting cast of characters. STORM OF THE POLITICAL CONTROVERSY SWIRLS AROUND KENNEDY VISIT the headline read. "President Kennedy wound up a day of 'non-political' campaigning in the Lone Star State with almost a hurricane of political controversy swirling around him," its lead began. As yet, neither man had turned the pages to see the scurrilous advertisement inside.

"Christ, I come all the way down here and make a few speeches, and this is what appears on the front page," Kennedy said first in disappointment. "I don't care if you have to throw Yarborough into the car with Lyndon. But get him in there." O'Brien promised to try to find Senator Yarborough. As Kennedy sat by the window, his feet propped up on the radiator, he looked out upon the rain-soaked parking lot where he would soon speak.

"Just look at that platform," he said, gazing down at the naked platform in the middle of the parking lot. "With all these buildings around it, the Secret Service couldn't stop someone who really wanted to get you."

It was a premonition that later took its place beside Lincoln's melancholy before a night at the theater, and Martin Luther King's talk of having been to the mountain before a demonstration in Memphis. It was the first of two Kennedy would have on this morning.

Just outside the lobby of the Texas Hotel, O'Brien had the good fortune to run into Yarborough almost immediately, and he made his case forcefully, as Yarborough groused. Perhaps the senator would issue a statement? Perhaps ... "You see that press bus over there?" O'Brien cut across him, gesturing across the parking lot. "We've come all the way down here, and you know what every one of those reporters is talking about? They're talking about you and Lyndon." Yarborough was "oversensitive," O'Brien said. He did not agree that Lyndon Johnson had stripped the senator of his appropriate patronage powers in the Senate.

"Well, if it means that much…" Yarborough grumbled.

"It does."

"Larry, I would do nothing to hurt the president, you know that," he replied, and the deal was struck. Now, O'Brien's only job was to make sure in Dallas that the promise was kept. He

Kennedy speaks in the rain. Behind: Senator Yarborough, John Connally, and LBJ

Jackie, Jack and LBJ at Fort Worth breakfast

went off and found Johnson shortly afterwards, and told him of Yarborough's reversal.

Soon the president emerged into the lobby. It was drizzling as he strode across the wet parking lot to address a stalwart and enthusiastic gathering. There are no faint hearts in Fort Worth, he began, as behind him Johnson, Connally, and Yarborough stood uneasily side by side at attention.

"Where's Jackie?" someone shouted.

"Mrs. Kennedy is organizing herself," Kennedy shot back. "It takes her a little longer, but of course she looks better than we do when she does it." The crowd laughed appreciatively.

On the way back in, Kennedy came face to face with Yarborough at the elevator. "For Christ sake, cut it out, Ralph," he said saltily. Yarborough was apologetic. The question was closed. But not quite. Moments later, as the president took his seat at the Chamber of Commerce breakfast in the Longhorn Room, he spotted Connally and summoned him over.

"John," said the president, "did you know that Yarborough refused to ride with Lyndon yesterday?"

"Yes, I heard about that last night."

"What's wrong with that fellow?" Connally did not know.

"By God, he'll ride with Lyndon today – or he'll walk," Kennedy said.

At the breakfast the rituals were soon under way. Upon this occasion the formalities had not been put through Connally's filter of Texas classiness, for exactly the wrong presents were bestowed upon the Kennedys as mementos of their visit: boots for Jackie and a Stetson for Jack. They took the gifts in good humor. Inevitably, the roar came from the crowd for the president to put on the hat. The president recoiled, but made a wisecrack of it.

"I'll put this on Monday in my office in the White House. I hope you can be there to see it."

*   *   *   *   *

In Dallas, Oswald wrapped his weapon in brown paper, and, when his fellow worker picked him up, he put the package in the back seat, mumbling something about curtain rods. It was not Oswald's practice to read the paper in the morning. But, if it were, he might have seen the story about the luncheon at the Trade Mart in the society pages the day before. Steak was on the menu, and a spokesman for the sponsoring organizations informed the press that the president's steak would be chosen at random. "Obviously, this is done for security reasons," he said cheerfully. "A would-be assassin couldn't be sure of poisoning the president's meal unless he put poison on every steak." Yet, Oswald had undoubtedly seen Wednesday's paper with the parade route and the news that the president and the governor would be riding in the second car.

The Kennedys arrived back in their hotel suite after breakfast for what might have been their last few minutes of privacy. Downstairs, Connally met the press to put out a few high-sounding homilies about party unity and to berate them for magnifying the feud between himself and Yarborough. His bland statement had been approved by President Kennedy. In Suite 850, Jackie Kennedy noticed for the first time that they were in the midst of a priceless art collection. Besides the Monet and the Van Gogh, there were a Picasso and a Prendergast, among others.

"They've just stripped their whole museum of all their trea-
sures to brighten up this dingy hotel suite," she said in a com-
pliment that Nellie Connally would have found backhanded.
From a catalog, which they had not seen the night before in
their haste and fatigue, Kennedy found the name of the orga-
nizer and called Ruth Carter Johnson, the wife of a newspaper
executive, to thank her. He then called for Lyndon Johnson,
and the vice president found Kennedy in an ebullient mood.
The enthusiasm of the drenched crowd in the parking lot had
brightened his spirits. He could go to a thousand Chamber
of Commerce functions, and they would mean nothing. But
when the people turned out in the rain spontaneously and
cheered, that meant something.

"You can be sure of one thing, Lyndon," Kennedy said
buoyantly, "we're going to carry two states next year, Massachusetts and Texas. We're going to carry at least two states!"

"We're going to carry a lot more than those two,' Johnson
replied, buoyant himself, for, if he had harbored a doubt over
whether he would be invited back on the ticket, it was swept
away now.

After Johnson left, the dour Kenneth O'Donnell came in
to dampen the fun. He had finally been shown the ad inside
the *Dallas News*, with its funereal black border, sarcastic head-
ing of welcome to the president, and sponsorship by H.L.
Hunt and Dallas Birchers. He'd registered its implications,
undisguised by its format of twelve rhetorical questions, that
Kennedy was secretly in league with American communists,
acquiesced in the Red imprisonment of Cuba, gave succor to

WANTED *EXhibiT - 4*

FOR

TREASON

THIS MAN is wanted for treasonous activities against the United States:

1. Betraying the Constitution (which he swore to uphold):
   He is turning the sovereignty of the U. S. over to the communist controlled United Nations.
   He is betraying our friends (Cuba, Katanga, Portugal) and befriending our enemies (Russia, Yugoslavia, Ppland).

2. He has been WRONG on innumerable issues affecting the security of the U. S. (United Nations-Berlin wall-Missle removal-Cuba-Wheat deals-Test Ban Treaty, etc.)

3. He has been lax in enforcing Communist Registration laws.

4. He has given support and encouragement to the Communist inspired racial riots.

5. He has illegally invaded a sovereign State with federal troops.

6. He has consistantly appointed Anti-Christians to Federal office: Upholds the Supreme Court in its Anti-Christian rulings.
   Aliens and known Communists abound in Federal offices.

7. He has been caught in fantastic LIES to the American people (including personal ones like his previous marraige and divorce).

CONFIDENTIAL

Flyer distributed before presidential visit

communist killers in Vietnam, persecuted his conservative critics. The advertisement was not easily dismissed, for it had been accepted by, and implicitly sanctioned by, the management of a major American newspaper.

The president handed it to his wife. "Can you imagine a newspaper doing that?" he said in disbelief. "We're headed into nut country now." It put him back into the melancholy of the morning. Dread and premonition were in the air.

"Last night would have been a hell of a time to assassinate a president," he said, gazing out of the window. "If anyone wants to shoot a president, it's not a very difficult job. All one has to do is get on a high building with a telescopic rifle, and there is nothing anybody can do."

There had been another piece, which Kennedy did not see. Several days before the president's arrival, A.C. Greene had written a column on the editorial page of the *Dallas Times Herald* entitled "Why Do So Many Hate the Kennedy's?" Three factors were listed, and the tone of

A.C. Greene column, Dallas Times Herald, *Nov. 20, 1963, three days before assassination*

Greene's editorial came close to legitimizing them.

First, Greene wrote, the Kennedys were rich with money that "stinks." "The Kennedy family is new rich and acts it. There is a touch of vulgarity in the way the Kennedy tribe lives." This vulgarity, he suggested, was made more obnoxious by their insincere attempt to act like real folks. In their arrogant hearts, "the Kennedys give the impression that ordinary people don't know how to think or act or do for themselves." Second was his religion, and third his civil rights program. The latter was especially infuriating, wrote Green breezily, because "the President isn't really as sincere in his civil rights pushing as he claims." Next to this discourse was a cartoon of Kennedy quaking as he stood before a huge smiling elephant marked Dallas, with the title "Profiles in Courage."

If a spark was needed to provoke some irrational nut into action, there were those in Dallas trying hard to provide it. That morning, five thousand cheap handbills were distributed bearing a presidential mug shot, as if it were a post-office "most wanted" poster: WANTED FOR TREASON was splashed across the top over jail-house mug shots of the president frontal and profile. But Oswald needed no jump-start. To a fellow worker Oswald asked with forced naiveté what all the commotion was about, and his comrade told him. Which way was the motorcade coming? Oswald asked. Along Houston Street to Elm. "Oh, I see," he said and turned languorously back to his work.

Meanwhile, in Fort Worth, Connally finished his press conference, satisfied that he had discharged his duty to the president on the subject of internecine warfare, and he sent word to him through Ken O'Donnell that Yarborough would be allowed, after all, to sit at an unstratified head table during the remaining functions.

"If the president wants Yarborough at the head table, that's where Yarborough will sit," Connally said magnanimously.

"Terrific," the president said. "That makes the whole trip worthwhile."

As he climbed the ramp to the plane, the clouds receded. His melancholy left him, swept away by his usually sunny disposition again, and by the cheers of the street crowd, as he rode to the Fort Worth airport for the hop over to Dallas. As the plane rose on its short parabola, Kennedy looked out the window at the improving weather.

"Our luck is holding," he said to Connally with a smile. "It looks as if we'll get sunshine."

Kennedy's buoyancy was infectious. When Connally emerged from the plane at Love Field behind the president and felt the sunshine, crisp and brilliant, he was filled with a sense of possibility and pride. The Connallys tarried by the limousine with Jackie Kennedy, her arms filled again with the inevitable roses. She did not find the midday sun and heat very comfortable: the temperature was already in the 80s, the infernal wind was up again, and she was sure she would swelter in her wool suit. As the president pumped hands at the airport fence, his traveling party watched the familiar scene languidly. Congressman Henry Gonzalez, who had felt as if a 250-pound weight had been lifted from his chest when the president left San Antonio safely, joked to his companion about his "steel vest." O'Brien kept a wary eye on Yarborough to make sure he didn't bolt. When Yarborough finally climbed into Johnson's car, the vice president did not acknowledge him but stared glumly forward under his cocked Stetson. Johnson would continue to stew all the way to Elm Street, never turning to Yarborough to say a word, much less a pleasantry, never turning to the sidewalk crowd, whose cheers were not for him. Yarborough put on a plastic smile, for he was enjoying the vice president's discomfort.

On the outskirts of the airport, the motorcade moved swiftly past scattered clusters of people. On a knoll, some distance from the roadway, a lone, disheveled, sour-faced figure stood by a battered Volkswagen, holding up a sign that read, YOU'RE NOTHING BUT A TRAITOR, but Kennedy didn't see it. By no means were all the political placards negative. One read, GOLDWATER IN 1864, KENNEDY IN 1964. With the president sitting directly behind the governor, the conversation in the president's limousine was sporadic and "desultory," as Connally would describe it. They eventually came upon another unfortunate sign, which read KENNEDY GO HOME and this time the president did see it.

"See that sign, John?" he said, leaning forward to Connally.

"I did but I had hoped you didn't," Connally replied, turning as best he could in his crunched-up position.

"I see them everywhere I go," Kennedy said, turning back to the crowd. "I bet that's a nice guy."

To Connally, the president seemed to be enjoying himself. At another point, when momentarily the crowds thinned, Kennedy leaned forward again.

"John, how do things look in Texas?"

"That *Houston Chronicle* poll should give us some ideas," Connally replied.

"What's it going to show?' the president asked, knowing full well from the night before what it showed.

"I think it will show that you can carry the state, but it will be a close election."

"Oh?" said the president, showing faint surprise, as Goldwater was ahead by four percentage points. "How will it show you running?"

"I think, Mr. President, it will show me running a little ahead of you."

"That doesn't surprise me," Kennedy said.

As the motorcade entered downtown, crowds grew into throngs, and when it turned onto Main Street, pointing down the canyon of sparkling glass and steel and granite, throngs became a multitude. Connally had never seen anything like it – many thousands of people packed into a space of a few city blocks. Its size far surpassed what San Antonio, Houston, or Fort Worth had produced. If he had felt before that he and only he could ensure the success of the president's trip, especially in Dallas, Connally was disabused of the idea now. These crowds were not for him. He was a mere passenger, a hanger-on, an appendage. He saw them as "restrained" in their enthusiasm, for this comported with his political expectation, but it was hard not to be swept up in the fantastic reception. Down the straightaway they went, flags fluttering, at a reasonable clip of about thirty miles per hour. At Houston, on the east edge of Dealey Plaza, the car slowed nearly to a stop to ease around the corner. By the courthouse, Nellie turned

"Dallas Loves You, Mr. President" - presidential security in 1963

to speak to the president in a tone full of excitement, full of pride in Dallas, in Texas, and in her husband for what *he* had just accomplished.

"Well, Mr. President, you can't say that Dallas doesn't love you!" she cried.

"No, you certainly can't," Kennedy replied with a smile.

In the shadow of the Book Depository, the car made its slow left turn onto Elm and started down the slope into the abyss. As they edged past a large tree, approaching the freeway sign, Connally's mind thrust ahead to the luncheon, only five minutes and an eternity away. The adulation was over.

At the crack of the rifle, he knew instantly what it was. His head turned sharply to the right, but he could not swivel his body that way because of the car's bulkhead, so he swung back

swiftly the other way, and then he felt the hammer strike his back. His swivel continued toward the left. His gaze fell on his lap, spattered with his blood. He was hit – badly – fatally, he supposed. His head titled skyward. "Oh, no! No! No!" he screamed, as he crushed the roses. "My God! They're going to kill us all!" The thought flashed through his mind that two or three men were out there, shooting with automatic weapons. Nellie's glance was riveted on him as she heard him scream. She reached out in horror, pulling him down into her lap. Her awareness grew with the milliseconds. The president was hit, too, she sensed, but he uttered no sound. He still sat strangely upright, a more distinct target now – indeed the only near-stationary target among other whirling bodies. He had upon his face a "quizzical look," his widow would later say, as if he was suffering from a "slight headache."

Oswald's first, wounding bullet had passed cleanly through the soft tissue of Kennedy's lower neck, missing the spinal cord and any bone, passing cleanly though Kennedy's necktie, then entering Connally's back, streaking through the governor's body, hitting his wrist and finally lodging in his thigh. When the bullet entered Connally's back, hitting bone, he pivoted in agony, first to his right, then forward, then to his left again in a contortion where he was almost looking directly backward at Kennedy. Eventually, his lithe body swiveled downward and ended up in Nellie's lap. In short, he was in constant, violent motion, writhing in terrible pain this way and that. Similarly, in those fateful six seconds, Jackie Kennedy was also in motion, leaning toward her husband as she sensed something was terribly wrong.

But because of the corset, the president's body moved only slightly. It was almost as if his torso was bolted to the back of the seat. His body did not act as a normal body would when a bullet passes through its neck. Only his hands moved to his throat, and his head jerked forward, but his torso stayed straight, erect and unmoving. Held by his back brace, Kennedy remained bolt upright for five full seconds. This gave the assassin time to reload and shoot again at a nearly fixed, unobstructed target.

The frames of the Zapruder film confirm this ramrod posture: Kennedy's head turns only slightly in those eternal seconds, and his upper body almost not at all, from frame 225 (when the first shot entered his neck) to the fatal frame 313.

Without the corset, the force of the first bullet, traveling at a speed of 2,000 feet a second, would surely have driven

Frame 312 of the Zapruder film, a millisecond before the killing shot.

the president's body forward, making him writhe in pain like Connally, and probably down onto the seat of his limousine, beyond the view of Oswald's cross hairs for a second shot. With no bones struck and the spinal cord intact, the president almost certainly would have survived the wound from the first bullet.

Then the killing shot landed, spraying the passengers with a fine mist. Connally knew what this was. Upon his trouser leg he saw a piece of blue brain, the size of his thumb, and he was a boy again, standing in a field not far from Floresville, with his father and one of the farm-hands, Carlos Estrada, next to a half-slaughtered steer hanging from a neighboring farmer's tree, and Estrada holding the precious blue brains that were the butcher's delicacy and his reward for unpleasant work.

Nellie held him. She now was the sole remaining stationary target. The car jerked slower as the driver instinctively hit the brake, contradicting his training. "Get out of line," Connally heard the agent-in-charge shout. "Get us to a hospital quick!" He did not hear Jacqueline cry out for her husband nor hear her scramble over the back seat. He heard only Nellie's comfort. "Be still now," she was saying. "Don't worry, you're going to be all right." She kept saying it over and over, beyond the point under the freeway where he lost consciousness.

"When you see a big man totally defenseless like that, then you do whatever you think you can to help," she was to say. "The only thing I could think to do was to pull him out of the line of fire. Maybe then they wouldn't hurt him anymore ... We must have been a horrible sight flying down that freeway with those dying men in our arms and going, no telling where.

We just saw the crowds flashing by. John said nothing. Once, I saw one little moment when [I thought] maybe he was still alive – and I kept whispering to him, 'Be still. It's going to be all right.'"

But she did not believe it. She thought he was dead.

CHAPTER NINE:

Parkland

n the parking lot of Parkland Hospital, the limousine screeched to a halt with a jerk that propelled Connally back into blurry consciousness. He knew that he lay across the jump seats and that the president had been hit, hit terribly. He had to get out of the way! With an extraordinary effort of will, he heaved himself out of Nellie's arms and tried to stand. He got nearly upright before the pain overcame him. "Oh, my God, it hurts! It hurts!" he screamed and collapsed. Men were running and yelling all around the vehicle. An agent shouted, "Get the president! Get the president!" In the back seat, Jackie Kennedy cradled her husband's head, covered now with the coat of a Secret Service agent. A figure of stone, immobilized by horror, she would not let go. They pulled at her husband, reaching over Connally's body, grabbing at that of the president. No, she would not let them have him. Agent Roy Kellerman's coat slipped down to the bridge of the president's nose, revealing the wasted cavity.

"You know he's dead. Let me alone," Jackie Kennedy muttered.

"Please, Mrs. Kennedy," the agent said solicitously, then firmly, "Please!"

Nellie Connally was overcome with a momentary bitterness. Amid the pandemonium, she seemed to be the only one concerned about her husband. Arms reached over his body toward the back seat, as she pleaded for attention. She knew the man in the back seat was dead. When someone finally reached in and began to help Connally out and onto a waiting stretcher, it seemed to Nellie as if they were doing so only to clear a path to the president. An orderly had hold of the governor's arms, and the president's pal, Dave Powers, shaking with sobs, grabbed Connally's legs.

Even in the horror and the pandemonium, protocol was observed. The gurney bearing the president was silent, his body limp. It went to Trauma Room #1. The gurney with Connally raced through the narrow, antiseptic passageway. The governor's body was tense, a good sign, as he roared with pain – his brain was functioning and intact. He was rushed into Trauma Room #2. Blood covered Connally's head. It was not his blood. Fingers pawed at his clothing. They were having trouble with his pants. "Cut them off!" Connally bellowed, and they did. In the hub of the emergency room, as Secret Service men with Tommy guns mingled wildly with doctors dangling the life-saving paraphernalia, Nellie Connally stood bewildered. She could hear her husband's leonine roar. After what seemed an eternity, someone rushed out and handed her one of his gold cuff links. What did it mean?

Professional hands were at work, as Bill Stinson, the governor's aide, rushed into Trauma Room #2. Dr. Red Duke had his hand under Connally's shirt, pressing hard against his chest.

"How is he?" Stinson said breathlessly.

"He's got a hole in his chest you could pack a baseball into," Duke said.

Stinson moved to the head of the stretcher. Connally was calmer now, almost composed, his eyes shut.

"Governor, can you hear me?" Stinson said softly in the governor's ear.

"Yes, Bill, I can hear you," Connally replied without opening his eyes.

"What happened?" the aide asked, smoothing the governor's ruffled hair.

"They shot us both, and I think they killed the president," Connally muttered.

"Where did the shots come from?"

"I don't know – but I think from behind."

"Is there anything I can do for you?"

"Just take care of Nellie," he said.

His pallor was ashen, due to the considerable loss of blood and to his difficulty in breathing, but his pulse was steady and his blood volume was adequate. He did not appear to be in shock. His wounds were terrible. On his right shoulder, in his back, a thumbnail's distance from the crease in the armpit, there was a regular, three-centimeter perforation. At an angle of thirty degrees downward, below the right nipple, there was a ragged five-centimeter wound. This was the "sucking wound" that Dr. Duke closed with his hand, and it, along with the possibility that the bullet had passed through the heart and the great vessels, represented the danger to Connally's life. Here, he enjoyed his first piece of luck. When Nellie had pulled him into her lap and held him, his arm had instinctively fallen across his chest and pressed against the wound, partially holding in his air and permitting him to breathe. The ride from Elm Street to the hospital had taken eight minutes. If it had taken more, he would have been dead. Then, there was another wound in his right wrist, and another in the thigh. For the moment, these were considered secondary. In the emergency room, the first impression was that the victim had been hit by two bullets.

An occlusive dressing was slapped on the sucking wound and pressed hard to control the escape of air and aid respiration, for the governor was, as his doctors later put it, "complaining bitterly" about his difficulty in breathing. His lung had collapsed – that much was clear. He was in danger of strangling to death. Expeditiously, the incision was cut between the second and third ribs, and a tube inserted into the lung to re-inflate it. The top thoracic and orthopedic surgeons in the hospital arrived, as the patient was prepared for surgery. Both Dr. Robert Shaw and Dr. Charles Gregory were veterans of World War II; between them they had experience with nearly 1,500 cases of bullet wounds. One floor above, the operating "suite" was readied. Dr. Shaw took a minute to explain to Nellie what needed to be done, and she authorized him to do whatever was necessary. As the gurney moved to its next station, Stinson trotted alongside Dr. Duke.

"Is he going to make it?" he asked.

"We won't know until we get him upstairs," the doctor replied grimly.

Upstairs, the gurney came to a stop next to the operating doors. As they lifted Connally off his stretcher to take him inside, something dropped from the stretcher to the floor. It was a bullet. A nurse picked it up and dropped it in her pocket. Inside, the governor was conscious enough to answer a few basic questions: When had he last eaten? Was he on any medication? Did he have any acute allergies? And then, at 1:07 P.M., thirty-two minutes after having been hit, he fell unconscious. He did so, the doctor later wrote, "without excitement."

Once the patient was put under sedation with sodium pentothal, Dr. Shaw proceeded to determine the full extent of the damage. The bullet had shattered ten centimeters of his fifth rib, the length of his middle finger. It had passed along the outer cusp of the rib and had splintered fragments inward, into the body, creating lethal "secondary" missiles. The shards of Connally's own rib, not the bullet, had collapsed the lung, perforating his bronchia. Thus, he was sucking air internally as well as externally. Upon further examination of the right wrist, it was determined that the damage, while great and delicate to repair, would have been considerably greater if the wrist had been struck initially, with the full force of the bullet. The last two similar wrist wounds that Dr. Gregory had attended had resulted in amputation. Hit by a bullet traveling at its full speed, 2,000 feet per second, a wrist would "literally be blown apart." In this case, it was apparent that

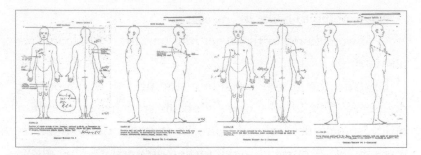

Clockwise, from top: Connally wounds; Schema of bullet path through Connally's body; Trajectory of bullets

the bullet had been largely spent, and from the nature of the laceration, had probably entered the wrist butt end first while it was tumbling. When Gregory finally turned his attention to the wound in the thigh, he found that it was a remarkably round puncture, stopping in the subcutaneous flesh and not passing into the muscle. Given its size and depth, about that of a pencil eraser, Dr. Gregory concluded that the butt end of the spent bullet had entered, and then dropped out.

The theory soon developed that a single bullet had caused the entire condition: entering his back, passing downward through the outer edge of the fifth rib, tumbling and exiting at the nipple, catching the wrist, then coming to rest in his left thigh.

If Lee Harvey Oswald had hit President Kennedy's brain dead on, he had missed Governor Connally's heart and great vessels by an inch.

Meanwhile, in an adjacent hallway, a dazed Congressman Henry Gonzalez drifted along behind Lyndon Johnson's aide, Cliff Carter, into a small, cramped side chamber of the emergency room. There, Johnson leaned against a doorway, saying nothing, frequently putting a sinus inhaler to his nose for a snort. Lady Bird stood nearby, blanched and quiet. Several other congressmen were present. Agent Kellerman of the Secret Service was shouting into a phone, apparently talking to the military command in Washington and assuring them in bursts of affirmations that he was with the vice president, and that Johnson was unhurt. Gonzalez still had no grasp of the situation. He did not know who had been hit. When he caught a glimpse of the president's limousine on the way into the hospital, he had seen the trampled and blood-soaked yellow roses of Texas and his first assumption was that Mrs. Kennedy had been the victim. No one told him differently now.

Cliff Carter came and went. In the hallway, the head nurse approached him, holding two grocery-store bags, containing Connally's clothes. The nurse wanted a signature on a form for their release.

"The governor is not expected to live," she said, bland as broth.

Carter entered the room and handed the two bags to Gonzalez. "Here, Henry, the governor's personal effects, you sign for them," he said, and then he was gone again. Gonzalez wandered out into the hallway, glad to have a pretext for leaving and having the vague intention of finding Nellie Connally and giving her the bags. Down the corridor he came to a dead end. To the right was the exit. He looked to the left, and there,

completely alone on a small
chair in an empty corridor
by the oak-paneled swinging
doorway to Trauma Room #1,
sat Jackie Kennedy. To Gonzalez, muddled about what
had happened, she looked
like a frightened rabbit. She
gazed at her hands, arranged
in her lap, still sheathed with
pink gloves that were caked
with blood. Gonzalez went
to her. Putting a comforting
hand gently on her shoulder, he said:

Senator Yarborough at Parkland.

"Mrs. Kennedy, can I get you a glass of water?"

She looked up and nodded. Down the hall, he found two
nurses who were locked in gossip and laughing raucous-
ly. Gonzalez asked for water. The nurses snapped that she
did not have any handy. Gonzalez ordered the water, and it
was grudgingly provided. "And this is no time for laughing,"
he scolded, as he turned back to the First Lady.

As he stood by Mrs. Kennedy, the door opened, and inside the room Gonzalez saw Mrs. Kennedy's press secretary, Pamela Turnure, and the president's secretary, Evelyn
Lincoln. Turnure smoked a cigarette. Between them was a
body, covered with a sheet. The soles of the feet were the only
flesh in view. Now he knew. Curiously, his Spanish tradition
flashed before him – a line from Gustavo Adolfo Bécquer's
Rimas: "How lonely are the dead..." Distantly, he heard Mrs.

Kennedy ask him for a cigarette. Fighting with himself, he took a few steps into the awful room to get a cigarette from Turnure. "No, it can't be. No, not here, it can't be," Gonzalez muttered to himself.

But it was. Behind those swinging doors to Trauma Room #1, a 28-year-old resident, Dr. Charles James Carrico, had received the president's body. As Kennedy's clothes were removed, Dr. Carrico noticed the back brace immediately. "It was white cotton or some fibrous support," he testified to the Warren Commission later, "with staves, bones, and, if I remember, buckled in front." Dr. Malcolm Oliver Perry, the senior surgeon on duty, was there within minutes, to supervise the case. He too took note of the back brace. "I pushed the Ace bandage which was wrapped around his waist and leg and pushed it up. He had no femoral pulse when I arrived." Within a half hour, Dr. Perry pronounced the president dead.

With no bones struck and the spinal cord intact, the president almost certainly would have survived the wound from the first bullet. Both Carrico and Perry testified to this likelihood (and apropos of the decades-long controversy, both testified that the small, round, clean wound in the front of Kennedy's neck was an exit wound rather than an entry wound). To Perry, the neck injury was "tolerable."

The president would have recovered. Because the bullet had passed below the larynx, the wound would probably not even have impaired his speech.

*   *   *   *   *

On the floor above, Nellie's friends were finding her. The

congressman from Houston, Jack Brooks, mustered a Texas version of the stiff upper lip. "Oh, he'll be out deer hunting at the age of ninety," he said cheerfully, not appreciating how poor a joke it was. Lady Bird Johnson had gone to Nellie. Of the two women she now must comfort, Lady Bird knew that both had recently experienced wrenching tragedies: Nellie with the suicide of her daughter, Kathleen, three years earlier; Jackie with the death of two-day-old Patrick three months before. In Nellie's face, Lady Bird perceived a tough determination.

As they fell into a long embrace, Lady Bird said, "Too much has happened. He's *got* to get well."

"He is, Bird. He's going to be alright," Nellie replied bravely. To many, later, the bravery of Nellie Connally in those first eight minutes was unsurpassed. It would be remembered that from the moment her husband was hit, she had pulled him into her lap, leaving herself exposed and stationary.

To go to Mrs. Kennedy was inexpressibly more difficult. What could one say? Jackie Kennedy and Lady Bird Johnson had maintained a courteous distance. They came from different cultures, different traditions; their men were very different, and they almost spoke different languages. Despite the correct and even occasionally warm feelings between them that accompanied official duties, they had each allowed their true feelings to pop through privately. Once Lady Bird had remarked patronizingly that Jackie Kennedy, unsophisticated as she was as a political woman, was a "girl born to wear white gloves." In turn, Jackie had once snapped, about Lady Bird's unquestioning loyalty to her husband, that Mrs. Johnson would walk naked down Constitution Avenue if Lyndon Johnson asked her to. Now in Dallas, all that was far from their minds. Lady Bird found Jackie composed "as a shadow."

"Jackie, I wish to God there was something I could do," she said.

No comfort was possible between Nellie and Jackie. In the pandemonium, as the doctors worked furiously on the governor and the casket was ordered for the president, the two women found themselves seated briefly together in the hallway, clad in nearly identical pink wool suits, both blood-spattered, only inches away from one another, yet one worlds luckier than the other. After some moments of silence, Mrs. Kennedy finally turned to Mrs. Connally, moving herself to inquire after the governor's condition.

"He'll be alright," Nellie replied stiffly. There was nothing she had to say or ask or offer in return.

At 1:35, almost exactly an hour after the horrendous insults to his body, Connally went into surgery. He had, of course, no comprehension of what was transpiring on the floor below: A priest insisting upon time-consuming formal pronouncements to the Almighty. A coroner standing upon the rules and threatening to block the removal of the president's body. Nurses insisting on the signing of endless forms. A youthful justice of the peace browbeaten by presidential assistants and shoved aside by gun-toting Secret Service men. An oak casket too heavy to be lifted by ordinary men, a press corps behind barriers clamoring for snippets of information. A blood-spattered widow. A country without a president. And his closest friend, Lyndon Johnson, seized with terror, thinking the assassination was the precursor to a Soviet nuclear attack. As Connally was under anesthesia, Johnson commandeered a police cruiser for the drive from the hospital to Love Field. The new president lay down on the floor of the back seat and ordered an officer to lie on top of him.

Even with the body of the president gone, terror still reigned at Parkland Hospital. How and why the shots were fired remained a giant mystery. Lee Harvey Oswald was still blithely riding Dallas city buses and easily hailing taxicabs as Connally went under the knife. Who had fired the shots? How many assassins were there? Was it an organized attack from abroad or a conspiracy from within? These questions were unanswerable, and that heightened the uncertainty and the terror. All that could be done at Parkland was to secure the place and make it certain that no more gunmen reached the governor in Texas.

To Bill Stinson, the governor's aide and the highest state official present at Parkland, his immediate duty was clear, even if his emotions were muddled. Should the governor die, there would need to be a transfer of power. Should more gunmen from this conspiratorial vanguard appear, the National Guard might have to be called out. Who would do it? How was it to be done? Stinson seized and secured a line to Austin and kept it open before he rushed to the operating room and demanded to be present during the governor's surgery. The chief surgeon began to object.

"You will not operate unless I'm present," Stinson ordered, and pushed him. "I am the senior state official here, and if power shifts, I need to know immediately."

Beyond Stinson's aggressive official posture, his dominant thought was about his friend and boss and mentor. He adored Connally. "My God, I may lose this dear man," he thought, and struggled to control himself. Clothed in surgical gown now, Stinson stood out of the way as the doctors opened Connally up. As the chest wound was exposed, Dr. Red Duke said in astonishment, "I've never seen *anything* like this."

*   *   *   *   *

Across the airwaves of Air Force One, known as *Angel*, where prominent figures were known in code, the radio traffic crackled with the terrible news. *Volunteer* was administered the oath of office, before *Angel* took off at 2:47 P.M. *Wayside*, with a planeload of cabinet members including Secretary of the Interior, Stewart Udall, on their way to Tokyo, had read the wire reports from *Crown*, and ordered the plane to turn back to Honolulu. *Watchmen* worried with *Witness* over whether a helicopter could even lift *Lancer's* heavy casket and take it to Bethesda. *Dagger* informed *Crown* that *Volunteer* would come immediately there and that *Victoria* and *Venus* would then proceed to Valley. *Warrior* talked with *Winner* about arrangements for the press upon arrival, when *Volunteer* would have a short statement. Then, blowing it all, *Tiger* told *Tanker* that President Johnson would deplane in the front of the aircraft upon arrival at Andrews.

Aboard Air Force One, the new president settled low in his seat, brows knit and eyes hooded, voice low, a man overwhelmed, grieving, and desperately concerned about the precarious life of his closest friend. There were a thousand affairs of state to attend to, and a few affairs of the heart, and toward the end of the flight to Washington he turned to the latter. He had to reach Mrs. Rose Kennedy. From the far distance of miles and culture, she was finally there on the line with this man who had replaced her slain son.

Echoing his wife, Johnson blurted out, in evident anguish, "I wish to God that there was something that we could do."

"Thank you very much," Rose Kennedy replied, curtly. "That's very nice. I know you loved Jack, and he loved you."

Lady Bird was also on the line, ever the standard of grace through these awful hours. "We're thankful that the nation had your son as long as we did," she said.

The Connallys remained uppermost in their minds. Surgery in the governor's chest was completed at 3:20 P.M., and somewhere over the middle South, Lyndon and Lady Bird watched a snowy television, as Dr. Robert Shaw came before the television cameras. Moments later, Angel was calling Parkland, and finally the plane was connected with Nellie Connally.

"We just heard some reassuring news over the TV," Lady Bird said. "We're up here in the plane. But the surgeon, speaking about John, was so reassuring…"

"The report was true," Nellie replied. "The surgeon who just finished said that John is going to be all right… unless something unforeseen happens."

Lyndon was there too. "Nellie, can you hear me?" he called down to her. "I love you. I know that everything's going to be all right….isn't it?"

"Yes," Nellie said, strong-voiced now. "Everything's going

to be all right."

"God bless you, darling," he said.

"Same to you."

"Give John a hug and a kiss for me," said the president.

"Good luck," Nellie replied, and she was gone. Actually, she had known for over an hour that her husband was likely to survive. Twenty minutes into the operation, the doctor told Stinson that the bullet had missed the great vessels, and the governor would live. He left and found Nellie, desolate and weeping, in the hallway. Kneeling in front of her in his surgical gown, taking both her hands in his, he said, "He'll make it," and she collapsed on his shoulder, "Thank God," she said.

Concern for the Connallys stabilized Lyndon Johnson in the coming hours. For Lady Bird, the Connallys represented more than the very closest friends they had. This catastrophe had happened in her state, and as a result her husband had acceded to an office he could never have attained on his own. His detractors were bound to cast this accidental elevation as some dark, medieval tale of regicide (as indeed it would be so cast in the play *MacBird*). Johnson called for Lady Bird's car at the White House and ordered her home. Her wise and irrepressible press secretary, Liz Carpenter, went with her.

"It's a terrible thing to say, but the salvation of Texas is that the governor was hit," Liz said.

"Don't think I haven't thought of that," Lady Bird replied, and then, gazing out into the miasma of a Washington night, "I only wish it could have been me."

At the White House Johnson ordered a television. Apart from the brief glimpses of television he had seen on Air Force

One, he had no perspective on the day's events wider than his own confined experience. Now, the romantic images of the handsome, athletic, well-born, graceful, martyred president flooded the screen: Kennedy and his small children vacationing at Hyannis Port – Kennedy at his inaugural with Robert Frost, the poet squinting against the cold January light, huddled against the biting chill, speaking of the dawn of a new Augustan age with power and poetry, where young ambition was eager to be tried – and Kennedy himself talking of the torch being passed to a new generation ... Kennedy ... Kennedy ... Kennedy.

"Let's turn that off," Johnson snapped. "I can't take this."

His actions were aimless. He read some wire copy and took no calls except one from his comforting ranch partner in Stonewall, Texas. He tried several times to get though to Connally's hospital room, but Bill Stinson was turning away all calls, and in any event the governor was still unconscious. One of the last things Johnson did before he retired for the night was talk again to Nellie Connally.

*   *   *   *   *

The following day, Saturday, the pattern continued. As Johnson vigorously seized the reigns of the presidency and began the transition of power, he found time to make repeated calls to Parkland. He spoke always to Nellie, because Stinson and the doctors forbade any direct calls to the governor, who lay groggily in a semi-comatose state. He flickered awake enough to notice for the first time that his arm was battened to a brace in traction above him. Until then, he had not known that his wrist and his thigh had been hit. In this twilight, he asked after Kennedy, and Nellie told him.

"I knew – I knew," he mumbled miserably this time. Some twenty members of his family had gathered at Parkland hospital. Texas Rangers, armed and nervous, guarded his door. They had reason to be nervous. Only later did it come out that Jack Ruby, the assassin's assassin, had mingled with the press on Friday at the hospital, merely a half-hour after the shootings on Elm Street.

On Sunday, Connally's first full day of consciousness, Oswald was shot and brought to Parkland. Ironically, Connally's aide, Bill Stinson, took charge of the emergency room as Oswald was brought in, and secured it with state patrolmen. In the course of the procedure, a reporter from the *Dallas Times Herald* was discovered hiding under a sheet beneath the gurney, and he was shooed out. Stinson watched as they worked to keep the killer alive. Compared to the gaping cavity in Connally's chest, Oswald had only a small perforation in his belly, but the eyes in his misshapen, sallow face never flickered open. Stinson watched, hoping for a deathbed confession, but it never came.

What had been let loose in America? No one was sure.

CHAPTER TEN:

The Conspiratorialists

Nearly three weeks after the assassination of President Kennedy, Connally began to tell his side of the story to authorities. On December 11, 1963, from his hospital bed in Austin (for he had developed an infection and had to be re-hospitalized), he gave his testimony to the FBI. From the beginning, his version differed in important details from the testimony of others.

"The first sense of anything unusual was when I became conscious of a shot, what sounded like a gunshot," he said. "Instinctively, I turned to my right, and as I did so, I sensed more than I saw, that President Kennedy was hit."

Here was a theory that was to become John Connally's alone: that Kennedy was hit by the first of Oswald's three shots. The second shot he reserved for himself.

"As I turned, I realized something was amiss with President Kennedy and then I turned back to my left, and as I did so I got hit with a bullet in my right shoulder."

The mortal blow exploded the president's skull. Even in his own agony Connally knew the shot was fatal, because he was spattered with brain tissue. The size of brain parts grew in subsequent renditions until it became the size of a man's finger. The shots were "unbelievably quick," he said, snapping the fingers.

By April of 1964 the President's Commission on the Assassination of President Kennedy (known unofficially as the Warren Commission, after its chairman, Chief Justice Earl Warren) was in full swing. Its central piece of evidence for sorting out the mystery of the three shots was the film from a home movie camera of a bystander on the grassy knoll named Abraham Zapruder. The central witness was John Connally. Both he and Nellie Connally were due to be questioned on April 21. A week beforehand, on April 14, the Commission staff met with ballistics experts and pathologists from the military to view the Zapruder film frame by frame. The conference resulted in a muddle. Perhaps the president and Connally

Connally leaving Parkland.

both had experienced delayed reactions to their wounds. "The President may have been hit as much as 36 frames (of the Zapruder film) before any visible reaction is seen," a memo on the meeting suggested. Both men may have been hit as many as two full seconds before the film shows any evidence of pain in their faces. If both bullets hit Connally, perhaps he only manifested a pained reaction to the second. The bullet that mysteriously dropped from Connally's stretcher was too perfect and intact to have passed through the bone of the wrist, the group asserted in what was probably its only definite conclusion, whether right or wrong.

Connally's surgeons at Parkland, Dr. Shaw and Dr. Gregory, were scheduled to appear before the Commission immediately prior to the Connallys. They came that morning with definite opinions about how their patient had been wounded, and this, of course, was what the Commission was hoping for. The doctors had spent considerable time with Governor Connally, rehashing the incident, and they had been influenced by his confident construction of the event. But before the doctors testified they were shown the frames of the Zapruder film, and it shook their certainty. To one Commission member, Allen Dulles of the CIA, Dr. Shaw confessed:

"Mr. Dulles, I thought I knew just how the governor was wounded until I saw the picture today, and it becomes a little harder to explain. I felt that the wound had been caused by the same bullet that came out the chest with the governor's right arm [held close to the chest]. This is still a possibility. But I don't feel it is the only possibility."

"Why don't you think it is the only possibility?" Dulles

asked.

"It is a matter of whether the wrist wound could be caused by the same bullet, and we [Dr. Gregory and myself] felt that it could. But we had not seen the bullets until today. We still do not know which bullet actually inflicted the wound on Governor Connally."

"Or whether it was one or two wounds?" Dulles interjected.

"Yes."

"Or two bullets?"

"Or three."

"Why do you say three?"

"He had three separate wounds."

"You have no firm opinion that all three wounds were caused by one bullet?"

"I have no firm opinion."

Dr. Charles Gregory, who had reconstructed Connally's wrist, cast further doubt on the one-bullet theory. Arlen Specter, the staff counsel of the Warren Commission, put the possibilities to Dr. Gregory. Certainly, one bullet could have caused all three of Connally's wounds, but what if that same bullet had first passed through the strap muscle of another man's neck? Could that projectile still cause Connally's wrist wound?

"I believe one would have to concede the possibility, but I believe firmly that the probability is much diminished," Gregory stated.

"Why do you say that, sir?"

"To pass through the soft tissue of the president would certainly have decelerated the missile to some extent," Dr. Gregory explained. "Having then struck the governor and shattered a rib, it is further decelerated. Yet it has presumably retained sufficient energy to smash a radius [of the wrist]. Moreover, [the bullet] escaped the forearm to penetrate at least the skin and fascia of the thigh, and I am not persuaded that this is very probable. I would have to yield the possibility."

Could the bullet have passed through Kennedy's back and the governor's rib and missed his thigh and wrist?

"I think that is a much more plausible probability," Dr. Gregory answered.

The combinations of possibility multiplied. Gregory had examined the pieces of bullet, other than the still well-shaped, intact bullet that had dropped from Connally's stretcher at Parkland. These were "grossly distorted" and such was the likely state of a bullet that smashed a wrist. Suddenly there was a new, even more grotesque possibility on the table: that the second bullet had penetrated Connally's chest, but fragments of the *third* bullet had ricocheted from Kennedy's skull, smashed Connally's wrist, and lodged in his thigh.

When Connally finally took the stand April 21, 1964, it was, in many ways, the climax of the entire Warren Commission deliberations. His views carried the weight and authority of prime survivor, as well as further authority: he was an experienced hunter who knew well the crack of a rifle shot. He, for one, would never mistake the sound for the pop of a firecracker or a motorcycle backfire, as had a number of policemen and even an army general on the scene. Yet his view was flawed by pain and delirium and even bitterness.

His testimony was riveting, "I heard this noise which I immediately took to be a rifle shot. Instinctively, I turned to my right, and I saw nothing unusual except just people in the crowd. I didn't catch the president in the corner of my eye. The only thought that crossed my mind was that this is an assassination attempt."

The beginning of his narrative was noteworthy for three things. He recognized it as a rifle shot and as an assassination attempt instantly. He turned to the right, and when he saw nothing, was in the process of turning back to the left. These very quick, rotating moves, like the juke of a basketball player, saved his life. If he had continued to turn right, to look all the way around over his right shoulder to President Kennedy, the bullet would have passed directly through his heart. Lastly, he never saw the president. He did not see him after the report of the first shot, which, after all, would have come to his ears after the bullet itself had found its mark. Thus, he had no basis for an opinion on whether the first bullet hit Kennedy.

"I never got far in my turn to the left. I was looking a little bit to the left of center and then I felt like someone hit me in the back. I knew I had been shot when I looked down, and I was covered in blood, and the thought immediately passed through my mind that there were either two or three or more people involved in this or someone was shooting with an automatic fire. These were the thoughts that went through my mind because of the rapidity of the two shots. I immediately assumed, because of the amount of blood, that I had probably been fatally shot."

Twenty-five years later, with a touch of irony, he would say that at that moment, he thought he was going to die. See-

ing his life flashed before his eyes, he was "not unhappy" with
what he saw. He did not elaborate, but seemed to be saying
that to be killed at this triumphant moment of his life and career, perhaps to be killed with a president who, in death, would
become the most popular president of the century, was not a
bad way to go. By implication, he might achieve for himself
the same lasting glory in his beloved Texas. But Connally's
awareness lasted longer. As he slumped down on Nellie's lap
he heard the third, fatal shot. He heard it clearly, he knew it
had hit the president, and it sounded louder. For it was – fig-
uratively, anyway.

"My God, they're going to kill us all," he had screamed. He
repeated it now for the Commission. It would be repeated
over and over in the years to come, as the rallying cry for the
conspiratorialists. For the Commission now, he permitted
himself only one brief, uncharacteristic lapse into survivor's
guilt.

"I have often wondered why I never had the presence of
mind [to say] 'Get down in the car!' but I didn't. You never
know why you react the way you do, and why you don't do
some things you ought to do."

Because Governor Connally had seen nothing, only sensed,
the Commission hoped the scientists and the technicians
could unravel the enigma. The Commission wanted to see the
wounds, and Connally obliged. He did more than that. There
had been confusing talk of exit wounds, of centimeters, and
dehumanizing medical jargon. Now, Connally said, "If the
committee would be interested, I would just as soon you look
at it."

John and Nellie Connally view the eternal flame.

He stood in the bland government hearing room, before his audience of buttoned up, flabby men, stripped off his shirt, and stood half-naked before them. The scars were terrible. What the bullet had done was awful enough, but the marks of the rapid surgical procedures – the stab of the scalpel, undertaken with speed to save his life by getting the tube in to re-inflate his lung, and then to expose the lung to remove the shrapnel of his own rib fragments – made the spectacle worse. Dr. Shaw had remained in the room for Connally's testimony. Now he was called upon to describe the scars, as if this was a Goya-like seminar for students in the medical arena.

"This scar does not look quite as nice as it does during the more lateral portion of the surgically induced incision, because his skin was brought together under a little tension, and there is a little separation there," he said clinically. In short, the scar looked like hell. Before it was over, Connally had also dropped his trousers, to show them the thigh wound.

Nellie Connally followed her husband to the stand. As a witness, she had advantages and disadvantages over Connally himself, although their versions were for the most part compatible. Her main advantage was her line of sight. The president had been diagonally to her right in the limousine, and she had just turned to him to say sweetly, "Mr. President, you can't say that Dallas doesn't love you."

Her disadvantage was that she had neither interest in guns nor experience in hunting. Now, she insisted, contrary to virtually every other witness and a mound of tangible evidence, that the first bullet passed through the president's neck, but not into her husband's back.

"I heard a noise and not being an expert rifleman, I was not aware that it was a rifle. It was just a frightening noise. It came from the right. I turned over my right shoulder and looked back and saw the president as he had both hands at his neck … He made no utterance, no cry. I saw no blood, no anything. It was just sort of nothing, the expression on his face, as he just sort of slumped down."

How fast had she reacted? The crack of the rifle shot came after the bullet had landed. Oswald's second bullet was in the chamber and being squeezed off. He could fire again in 2.3 seconds. Was the commission to believe that this genteel lady had had an instantaneous or a delayed reaction to this unfamiliar sound? Indeed, the reaction time of three passengers in the limousine now moved to the center of the investigation. The Commission went back to the ultimate source, the Zapruder film.

As central as the film was, it had one critical void. As the presidential limousine came down Elm Street, a road sign had obscured President Kennedy and Governor Connally from view, apparently at the very moment when the bullet or bullets found their mark. The film had to be analyzed frame by frame. Eighteen frames make up a second of time, and the principals are out of view for less than a second. The limousine and its passengers pass from view at frame number 206. Cramped with his knees against the front seat and his right side against the bulkhead of the car, Connally comes back into view at frame 223. He is lurching to his right. Kennedy reemerges at frame 225. His right hand is at his chest level, moving rapidly towards his throat. He is hit. The hand arrives at the throat at frame 227.

Connally now told the Commission, after he studied the film, frame by frame, that he thought he was hit somewhere between frames 231 and 234, or one-third of a second later than Kennedy. On the basis of that arithmetic alone, Nellie Connally's version – that the first bullet hit Kennedy and the second hit Connally – was impossible, for it took a minimum of 2.3 seconds or 41 frames of film for the same rifleman to shoot, reload, and fire again. It was impossible – unless there was more than one shooter, multiple men firing simultaneously from the same place. It came down to how fast and in what manner Kennedy and Connally reacted to their wounds. Kennedy's reaction was shown by his hand, Connally's from the swivel of his body.

The debate had shifted into the vague area of prompt or delayed reactions, both by the wounded men and by the witnesses. There is no science to it. Some doctors maintained that the reaction to a wound in the neck that hits no bones might be more delayed than the reaction to a wound, which shatters a rib and collapses a lung. This was the position of Dr. Robert Shaw.

"There can be a delay in sensory reaction," he testified to the Warren Commission, "an extended sensation, then just a gradual building up of a feeling of severe injury. But in the case of a wound that strikes a bony substance such as a rib, usually the reaction is quite prompt."

If Kennedy and Connally were hit by the same bullet – the second – and Kennedy's hand went to his neck before Connally screamed in evident pain as he felt the punch in his back, how could this be? The conspiratorialists quickly offered the opinion that the men were hit by two separate bullets that landed at virtually the same millisecond. Not everyone felt as Dr. Shaw did. Bill Stinson, Connally's administrative aide, for example, had been a rifleman in World War II and had had his elbow shattered by shrapnel in combat. Stinson remembered his own delayed reaction had been considerable, for he had not realized he had been wounded until he could not lift his arm and aim his rifle at the onrushing enemy. Contrary to Dr. Shaw's testimony, other doctors would testify to the Commission that delayed and indeed nonexistent reactions to wounds were not uncommon.

Ironically, twenty years later, in another assassination attempt on a president, the subject of delayed reaction was again a factor. For a full *fifteen minutes*, not until Ronald Reagan was in the Trauma Room of George Washington Hospital and the doctor noticed a small perforation under his arm, was it understood that the president had been shot. In the confusion after Hinckley's shots, it was several minutes before Reagan felt pain, and then it was assumed that he was having a heart attack, for he exhibited the classic symptoms of that condition. Later, it was finally appreciated that Hinckley's bullet had struck the limousine first, had flattened itself like a dime, and had entered the president's body tumbling, collapsing his lung, and coming to rest in the shadow of his heart. The threats to Connally's and Reagan's lives, therefore, were remarkably similar medically.

On April 21, Connally and his surgeons left the Commission with an unsolved mystery. But on May 6 a very different set of doctors, the forensics experts from the Wound Ballistics Branch at Edgewood Arsenal in Maryland, clarified the matter. They were led by the chief of the Wounded Ballistics Branch at Edgewood, Dr. Alfred Oliver, a veterinarian in training. The commission had ordered these experts to make ballistics tests simulating the wounds to Connally and Kennedy.

At the Commission hearing of April 21, Dr. Oliver had talked at length with Connally's surgeons, and he had received the X-rays and operative reports from Parkland Hospital. Consistent with established procedures, Oliver then conducted tests on a goat dressed in a suit, a shirt, and an undershirt, and also on a human cadaver, by firing bullets from a Mannlicher-Carcano rifle into the same places Kennedy and Connally had been shot. Working backward from Connally's wrist wound, the Edgewood test determined that the governor's wrist could not possibly have been struck by a "pristine" bullet (or one which had not encountered some interference before its impact). Oliver concluded that the damage to Connally's wrist would have been considerably greater if the bullet had passed through only his chest and then into his wrist. Such a missile would still have had "terrific penetrating ability" and considerable "wounding potential." Most significantly, the entry wound in Connally's back – three centimeters in diameter – did not indicate a pristine bullet either, but one which was yawing or wobbling on its axis.

What could cause such a thing? At Edgewood, the team positioned a piece of horse meat, equivalent in density to the boneless portion of the human neck, and then fired through it into the well-dressed goat. With this configuration, they found the velocity of the bullet reduced by 200 feet per second as it passed through the horse meat, and it took on a yawing motion, passing through the goat's rib and doing an equivalent amount of damage to a simulated wrist as Connally's has suffered. To the Commission, or more specifically, to four out of seven of its members, this was the proof of the single bullet theory. This theory was bolstered by the absence of any damage to the seats of the presidential limousine from a bullet that might have penetrated the president's neck, but somehow missed Connally altogether. If it had so missed, it would have had to lodge in the upholstery of the car.

John Connally would never accept it. Not in 1964, not three years later when he wrote about it for *Life* magazine, not fifteen years later when he testified again about it before a select committee of the House of Representatives. He argued his singular position with a fervor that went beyond any possible supporting facts, as if it were a point of vanity that Lee Harvey Oswald had reserved a special bullet for him. His visceral aversion to the notion that he shared a bullet with Kennedy was clear. By November 1966, a week before the third anniversary of the calamity, the Warren Commission was under serious attack.

There are two footnotes worth mentioning in this complicated tale. First, there was apparently some consideration in the Warren Commission of the possibility that Connally was, indeed, Oswald's real target. On January 30, 1964, Warren Commission assistant counsel, David W. Belin, wrote a memo to chief counsel J. Lee Rankin, entitled "Oswald's knowledge that Connally would be in the presidential car and his intended target." Many years later, Belin would say that the Commission rejected the possibility on the "common sense" grounds that if Connally was the target, Oswald would have fired as the presidential limousine approached the Book Depository rather than when it had already passed the building, and that Oswald had numerous other opportunities to kill Connally as the governor made public appearances around the state.

There are answers to these objections. Oswald was not a stalker like, say, Governor Wallace's assailant, Arthur Bremer, and he did not have the funds to run all over the state after Connally. Moreover, the governor's travel schedule was not a matter of wide public knowledge. On November 22, Governor Connally, with President Kennedy, was coming right past the building where Oswald worked. In addition, in the so-called "Nixon Incident," Oswald may well have strapped his revolver to go after Connally as Connally was publicized to be in Dallas speaking to a space conference.

As for Oswald not shooting when the vehicle approached the building, this projects the discussion into the speculative realm of the criminal mind. For instance, Oswald may have felt he had a better chance of getting away if he fired after the vehicle was already past his sniper's nest than when it was approaching. Psychologists speak of a "motor program" that takes place in the mind of a person in a high state of excitement and anxiety, especially a life-and-death situation. Oswald was in such a state. In a "motor program," the person cannot be asked to make precise, intelligent judgments about fine points of reason and logic. Once, in those terrible seconds, he began to execute his plan to murder, he could not distinguish between Connally and Kennedy; he could only keep firing. And for the second fatal shot, only the president remained as a virtually stationary target. It may be less important what Oswald was feeling and doing in the split seconds before he pulled the trigger than what was in his mind two days before the assassination when he settled upon his intention.

The second footnote deals with the January 30, 1961 letter that, as Secretary of the Navy, Connally had received from Lee Harvey Oswald about the change in his discharge from the Marine Corps from honorable to dishonorable – the letter that may well have been the catalyst for the entire assassination tragedy. According to Connally's aide at the time, Captain Andy Kerr, Connally had, in fact, paid considerable attention to Oswald's letter when it was first received.

"Connally called me to ask a couple questions about the Oswald case, which seemed to interest him," Kerr wrote, "He [felt] that the case had overtones which he wanted to be sure to understand. But after talking about it, he agreed that a referral to the Commandant [of the Marine Corps] which was basically a kiss-off, was the way it should be handled." When Connally came to Washington to testify to the Warren Commission, he made a special trip to the Navy Secretary's office and asked for the original letter. Kerr looked for the letter in the Navy's files, but could not find it, because, of course, it had been sent to the Warren Commission. Three years later, Connally again tried to obtain the original of the catalytic letter for his estate, using LBJ's press secretary, George Christian, as his intermediary to make a formal request to the National

Archives. By 1967, the artifacts of the assassination had taken on considerable financial value, and the Archivist eventually felt that Connally's instinct was mercenary.

"Should we do this for Governor Connally?" a memo to the Archivist of the United States read. "To do so might cause requests from other people such as Marina and Marguerite Oswald for free copies of other letters written by Oswald to the government."

The Archivist of the United States said no.

*   *   *   *

The stock of the conspiracy industry is trading high. Nearly three dozen books and articles have been published challenging the Commission's conclusions. While the Warren Commission concluded definitively and correctly that Oswald acted alone, the various conspiracy theories about the famous Grassy Knoll have been thoroughly discredited by painstaking historical research. No convincing evidence of a conspiracy has ever come forward. Yet, a 2012 History Channel poll found that more than 85% of the American people now believe there was a conspiracy in the death of President Kennedy.

But what foreign government, Cuban or otherwise, would stick with a designated assassin after he had blown his cover in the attempt on General Edwin Walker's life? And what foreign government or professional criminal organization would provide their assassin with a cheap mail-order rifle like Oswald's Mannlicher-Carcano with low-grade, jacketed ammunition instead of a high-quality rifle with the best sights and expanding ammunition? And how could these supposed

sponsors of assassination know in advance that with its ev-
er-changing plans for a presidential motorcade, a presidential
limousine would pass beneath the very window of the building where Lee Harvey Oswald had been employed for several months? In short, what government or mobster would
entrust so horrendous an act as presidential assassination to a
volatile, unreliable character like Oswald?

In this wholly unsupported embrace of conspiracy, public
opinion reflects the political judgment of the Warren Com-
missioners that there had to be a motive as earth-shattering as
the murder itself. The assassin remains a mystery man. There
are Oswald doubles and magic bullets and whitewashes. The
testimony of Governor Connally and his wife, Nellie, became
the chief source of succor and encouragement to those alternative theories. Few now seem willing to countenance the truth
that the key to the greatest crime of 20th-century American
history can be found in the loose wires and weak connections
in the confused mind of a pathetic American outcast.

For a time in 1966, Mark Lane's book, *Rush to Judgment*,
stood atop the bestseller list. His chapter entitled "The Magic
Bullet" made a farce out of the Commission's theory of the
single bullet that wounded both men. Connally's testimony
was the centerpiece of Lane's argument. Edward J. Epstein's
book, *Inquest*, also published in 1966, was a more solid challenge. He reported that three of seven Commission members
– Senator Richard Russell, Senator John Sherman Cooper,
and Congressman Hale Boggs – believed that there might
have been separate bullets. Unquestionably, the debate within
the Commission over the wording of the final description of

the single-bullet theory was spirited. "Compelling" was in the first draft. "Credible" was Senator Russell's proposal. "Persuasive" appeared in the final draft. "The Governor flatly stated that he knew that the bullet that hit the President could not have been the one that struck him," Lane wrote. In fact, Connally had said no such thing three years before. He had not stated a certainty at all, but merely an impression, gleaned from a sixth sense, about events that took place behind his back.

In 1966, however, Connally made a gentleman out of Mark Lane. After a silence of three years, Connally agreed to examine the Zapruder film for *Life* magazine. Of the theories in the wind, Connally asserted now with a boldness that verged upon arrogance, "As far as I'm concerned, there is no 'theory.' There is my absolute knowledge – and Nellie's too – that one bullet caused the president's first wound and then an entirely separate shot struck me."

"No one will ever convince me otherwise," Nellie said.

"It's a certainty. I will never change my mind," Connally added.

Life magazine used the Connally analysis to sound the call for a new commission of inquiry. The conspiratorialists howled with delight. Connally had made their inferences into a declaration of belief and conferred upon them a dignity and authority they previously lacked. His testimony became their point of departure. Connally wanted it both ways. He wanted his two-bullet theory, and yet he recoiled at the notion of being in league with the likes of Mark Lane. The press clamored for a clarification, and on November 23, 1966, Connally gave one. In his opening statement, he expressed shock at "journalistic scavengers" like Lane, who attempt to "impugn the motives of the [Warren Commission] individually, cast doubts upon the Commission as a whole, and question the credibility of the government itself." But no one witness had been more important to Lane's argument than Connally, and now Connally did not shrink from his two-bullet "certainty."

In Lyndon Johnson's White House there was consternation at Connally's flamboyant challenge. As Connally proclaimed his desire not to fan the flames, his statements became veritable bellows. Senator Richard Russell, one of the doubting Commission members, finally went public with his misgivings. In an interview with an Austin paper, Russell declared his agreement with Connally on the one-bullet/ two-bullet question, and cast doubts on other important elements of the Commission's conclusions: the absence of a conspiracy, whether the Soviet Union had disclosed everything about Oswald's activities there between 1959 and 1962, and whether the Commission knew everything about Oswald's Cuba-related activities. Senator Russell Long, whose father, Huey, had been the victim of assassination, said, "whoever fired that second shot was a better shot than Oswald." Even Malcolm Kilduff, who acted as Lyndon Johnson's press secretary in Dallas, told the press now that he agreed with Connally's rather than the Commission's version of the second bullet. The brickbats came from the most unlikely redoubts. The historian Arthur Schlesinger, Jr., joined *Life* magazine in a call for a new Commission.

The White House wondered what to do. In a top-secret

memo to Johnson, presidential adviser Jack Valenti, just back from Europe, reported widespread disbelief in the Warren Commission findings and suspicion of either blundering or a cover-up. The consensus in Europe was that Oswald had not acted alone.

"This is not a lightly or rarely held view," Valenti wrote. "It is widening among the peoples of Western Europe. It could become so malignant as to threaten seriously the very integrity of the American Government." Valenti proposed a counter-attack on the mountain of criticism by a distinguished panel of lawyers, headed by Louis Nizer. "Nizer and others sought to be unleashed *immediately* to publish a counter defense that would nail the detractors and the irresponsible nuts to the wall. The key to the whole assault on the Commission is the so-called single bullet theory. If this panel of distinguished lawyers could demolish the attack on the single bullet theory, the slanderers would be laid to rest."

Of course, Valenti was requesting LBJ to launch an attack, in essence, on his closest friend, John Connally, who might in that memo be considered a detractor at the least, and a slanderer and nut at worst. Nothing came of it. In his November 23 press conference, Connally said only that he had had "casual conversation" with Johnson about the Commission findings.

Presidential consultant John P. Roche was more pointed about Connally. "The comments of Richard Russell and the *Life* magazine article by Governor Connally are the two most serious blows which have yet occurred to the public credibility of the Warren Commission," Roche wrote to the president. "Paranoia is more infectious than measles. We have enough problems already with the war in Vietnam. To have the nation suddenly indulging in an orgy of sick speculation on events in Dallas could really poison the atmosphere." But attacks on the Commission could no longer be ignored, Roche wrote. He knew only what should not be done: the president should *not* reconvene the Warren Commission, and he should *not* appoint another Commission. In the end, Connally himself suggested the course of action to Johnson that the president should take a gentlemanly distance from the tempest that he, Connally, was causing.

Mark Lane, meanwhile, basked in the glory Connally had conferred upon him. He seized the moment to release a new chapter to his bestseller, which was about to be published in France. In the new material, Lane unveiled a five-bullet hypothesis: the first to Kennedy's neck, the second to Kennedy's neck *from the front*, the third to Connally's back, the fourth to the street, and the fifth the mortal wound to the president's head. His "facts," he claimed, showed *conclusively* that bullets flew from two directions. Of Connally's *Life* article and press conference, Lane said, "Governor Connally displayed an abysmal ignorance of the implications of his own testimony. If the bullet that struck President Kennedy did not also strike Governor Connally, then there was no lone assassin."

In this point anyway, the old scavenger was dead right.

For twenty-five years, Connally's first horrible words as he was hit: "My God! They're going to kill us all!" have remained the rallying cry for the conspiratorialists.

*   *   *   *   *

On February 11, 2013 I traveled out to the National Archives in College Park, Maryland, taking with me Dr. Lawrence Altman, the long-time medical correspondent for the *New York Times* and my colleague at the Woodrow Wilson International Center for Scholars. It had been a struggle to get the Archives to agree to let me see the corset that the president was wearing on November 22, 1963. One had to have a good scholarly reason as to why looking at the picture of it was not enough, for, appropriately, the Archives was intent to resist the voyeurism that sometimes surrounds the Kennedy assassination. My reason was that I need to see the actual brace to evaluate the stiffness of the plastic disc in the back of the brace that covered the president's sacrum and further bolted him upright in his seat on that day.

Two archivists brought the artifact to the antiseptic viewing room in a pristine wooden box. Opening it carefully, as if they felt the weight of history, and then putting on white gloves, they lifted the tan corset out and laid it on the table. I asked them to measure it and put my wide palms over my own midsection to imagine how complete the grip of the thing was. And then they spread out the wide Ace bandage that had been wrapped over the corset. If in developing my theory about the psychological importance of Oswald's military discharge I was channeling my own military service and remembering how much I valued my own honorable discharge, now I was referencing my experience as a pretty good, but often injured college athlete and the many times I had used an Ace bandage to hold my bruised and battered body together. It was almost beyond imagining how tight that corset and Ace bandage ensemble must have felt, as the president went out in public. I wondered how he stood it. One of the archivists pulled out the plastic disc from its envelope in the back of the brace. I did not want to touch it.

The author views JFK's corset at the National Archives, February 2013

In past projects I had felt before the detritus of history. I had handled the transcript of Galileo's interrogation by the Inquisition. I had watched a North Carolina prison director snake the tubes of a lethal injection apparatus between his fingers as we talked about a female prisoner he was about to execute. I had walked the walls of crusader castles when I was writing about the Third Crusade of Richard the Lionheart and Saladin....and waded through the tall grass around the pavilion of Jonestown, littered with toys and baby bottles.

But there was something different about this "damned girdle" as the late Senator Yarborough had called it in our conversation 25 years ago. This is as close as I ever want to get again to the quintessence of tragedy.

THE END

Notes on Chapter One:
The Assassin

Oswald's plan to defect: *Fort Worth Star Telegram*: November 1, 14, and 15, 1959.

Oswald's diary: WC, vol. 16, CE 24.

Oswald in the American Embassy: Richard Edward Snyder and John A. McVickar, testimony, WC, vol. 5. Oswald's demeanor in his first appearance at the Moscow Embassy suggested to Snyder that this was the young man's "big moment in history" and that if he could stall him, Oswald would not be emotionally ready for a second performance in a few days.

Potential intelligence damage of Oswald's defection: John E. Donovan, testimony. WC, vol. 8

Oswald's renunciation: It remains one of those ironies in history that, had the American consul, Richard Snyder, not been so sensitive about the perils of precipitous emotional renunciation of citizenship, Oswald would never have been permitted to reenter the United States. The author subscribed to this position, despite a letter Mr. Snyder wrote to the editor of *Time* magazine, after my cover story appeared in *Time* on November 25, 1988. Snyder contends as a technical matter that even if Oswald had succeeded in formally renouncing his citizenship, he could have obtained an immigrant's visa to return to "the land of his birth." The author believes that, given Oswald's fractured emotional state of mind in 1962, he never would have pursued the bureaucratic wrangles that the application for an immigrant's visa would necessarily have entailed. (Richard E. Snyder, letter to the editor, *Time* magazine, December 1, 1988.)

Letter to Robert Oswald: November 26, 1959, WC, vol.16, CE 295.

Russian attitude toward Oswald: Yury Nosenko (a KGB officer who later defected to the West), references in WC, including Commission document 451, his interview by FBI. March 4, 1964; see also summation of the Nosenko testimony, House Assassinations Committee report, p.101.

Oswald's life in Russia: His "historic" diary, WC, exhibits 24 and 101.

Letter to Robert Oswald: July 14, 1961, we, vol. 16, CE 301.

Oswald's confession of MVD supplement: WC, CE 25.

Marguerite Oswald letter: WC, CE 25.

The entire Oswald discharge file: WC, vol. 19, Folsom Exhibit 1.

Notes on Chapter Two:
Repatriation

Bouhe's charity: George Bouhe, testimony, WC, vol. 8.

Oswald's antipathy to Connally: Alexandra de Mohrenschil-dt (Mrs. Donald Gibson), WC, vol. 11.

Oswald as welder: Tommy Bargas, testimony, WC, vol. 10.

Oswald at Jaggars-Chiles-Stovall: John G. Graef, WC, vol. 10.

Notes on Chapter Three:
The Turning

General Walker assassination attempt: *Dallas Morning News*, May 11, 2013.

Warren Commission dismissal of "Nixon Incident": WC Report, pp.175-176.

Connally's appearance in San Jacinto: *Dallas Morning News*, April 21, 1963.

Oswald's speech in Mobile: WC, vol. 25, CE 2649. Exhibit 2648 comprises two letters from Oswald's cousin, Eugene Murrett, one before his Mobile lecture and one afterwards. The August 22, 1963, letter shows that Oswald's speech was taken seriously and was a success. Also see FBI interview with Father Malcolm P. Mullen, S.J., professor of philosophy at Spring Hill College, who attended the Oswald lecture (WC, CE 2649). The actual quotes from Oswald's appearance come from a summary provided to the FBI by Robert Fitzpatrick, S.J., also contained in CE 2649.

Oswald's radio interview in New Orleans: WC Vol. XXI, Stuckey Exhibit No. 3

The Oswalds' attitude toward Kennedy: McMillan, *Marina and Lee*, p. 333. De Mohrenschildt autobiography: In House

Assassinations Committee supplementary material. References to Oswald's admiration of Kennedy are on p.132.

Oswald as an agent to state violence: Partly from his own training in U.S. Army intelligence in the recruitment of covert intelligence agents, the author believes firmly that the notion of recruiting such an undependable agent as Oswald for assassination is absurd. If Cuba or the Soviet Union had wanted to assassinate an American president, they had far more reliable instruments of violence than Oswald.

Notes on Chapter Four:
Roads Taken Reluctantly

Connally's treatment of the Texas trip: *Life,* November 22, 1967, and his testimony to the House Assassinations Committee, 1979.

Oswald's trip to Mexico City: For this and in much else that applies to Oswald's state of mind, I have relied on McMillan's book, *Marina and Lee.*

Oswald in Austin: Lee Dannelly, FBI interview, WC Exhibit 2137. William Stinson, interview with author. As Governor Connally's aide, Stinson confirmed that attempts were made to verify Oswald's presence in Austin after the assassination, but the effort did not appear to go much beyond checking to see if Oswald had signed the governor's guest book. The *Texas Observer* also wrote about this possibility, December 27, 1963.

Dallas loves Connally: William Stinson, interview with author.

Connally loves Dallas: William Manchester, interview with author. In his interview with Connally for his book *The Death of a President,* Manchester was horrified at Connally's undemocratic instincts; the governor's attitude toward Dallas politics was the prime example. Connally's elitist instincts fit perfectly Manchester's definition of a fascist; Manchester believed that the American system was intended to exclude politicians like Connally.

Skelton's letters: Part of the reason why Skelton's letters about danger in Dallas were dismissed is, in my view, that he was arguing his own special interest so passionately. He wanted Kennedy to attend the dedication of the Stillhouse Hollow Dam on Lampasas River during the President's visit to Texas, because the dam was in his Central Texas region. On May 17, he wrote to Johnson's aide Cliff Carter:

"It will be recalled that the President and the Vice President were elected by the great Central Texas area extending from Beaumont to Abilene and from Dallas to Austin by a narrow margin of 45,000 votes. Bob Poage's [the powerful congressman from Waco and chairman of the House Agriculture Committee) district alone contributed 15,000 of those votes. They did not carry Fort Worth, Dallas, San Antonio or Houston, and yet these cities have received practically every major appointment under this Administration. There is considerable dissatisfaction and grumbling here over this fact, and if we are now by-passed in preference to the Republican cities, which voted against us, it will be more than serious."

Fulbright as Cassandra: Senator William J. Fulbright, interview with the author.

Connally's meeting with congressmen: Connally testimony before House Assassinations Committee, 1979; Henry Gonzalez, interview with the author.

Oval Office conversation between Kennedy and Connally: Connally testimony before House Assassinations Committee, 1979.

Notes on Chapter Five:
A Lead Unexplored

Jarnagin: The entire dialogue that Jarnagin transcribed in contained in the Warren Commission file as Exhibit 2821. Through an attorney in San Antonio, the author also made a discreet check on Jarnagin's reputation. Jarnagin interview with author.

Robin Hood: Shirley Ann Mauldin, FBI interview, December 9, 1963, WC, Henry Wade, testimony, WC, vol. 5, and interview with author; Jarnagin, interview with author.

Press conference of Dallas district attorney, Craig Watkins: *New York Times*, Feb. 19, 2008

Henry Wade: testimony, WC, Vol. 5, and interview with author.

Jarnagin's polygraph test: John F. Kennedy Archive, Dallas City Archives, Box 13, Folder 4, Item 45 - Polygraph Transcript, by P. L. Bentley., (Photocopy), 03/02: /64.

Jarnagin remark after failing the test: Aynesworth, Hugh, *JFK: Breaking the News*, International Focus Press, 2003, p.217, 231]

Notes on Chapter Six:
Trade-Off

LBJ attitude towards a possible Cuban conspiracy: In Johnson's CBS interview with Walter Cronkite, September 23, 1969, Johnson was asked about a possible international conspiracy behind Oswald. He replied: "I can't honestly say that I've ever been completely relieved of the fact that it might have been international connections," he replied.

"You mean you still feel that there might have been?" Cronkite asked.

"Well, I have not completely discounted it."

"What direction does your lingering suspicion lead you? To Cuba? Is that the area that you feel might have been involved?"

"Oh, I don't think we ought to discuss suspicions because there is not any hard evidence that led me to the conclusion that Oswald was directed by a foreign government or that his sympathies for other governments could have spurred him on his effort. But he was quite a mysterious fellow, and he did have a connection that bore an examination. [On the] extent of the influence of those connections on him, I think, history will deal with much more than we are able to now."

Upon the advice of Johnson's staff, this interchange was specifically cut for "national security" reasons from the CBS broadcast; (Bob Hardesty memo and Mildred Stegall memo, April 28, 1975, LBJ library).

A real agent of state assassination: For a contrast to Oswald, see the report of the Church Committee hearings, U.S. Senate, in 1975 on the subject of "Alleged Assassination Plots involving Foreign Leaders." Particularly interesting is the section on Cuba and the American agent called AM/LASH, a high official in the Cuban government, who was being groomed for a possible assassination attempt on Castro, and who was being provided with poisoned cigars, poisoned pens, and other instruments of assassination.

The Church committee established that Allen Dulles, later one of the Warren Commission members, knew about the plots to assassinate Fidel Castro, which were being developed within the CIA. It would not have been a huge leap of psychology for Dulles to assume that the Castro government was plotting an assassination in the same way.

On page 72 of the Church Committee report, there is this sentence: "The most ironic of these [American assassination] plots took place November 22, 1963 — the very day that President Kennedy was shot in Dallas — when a CIA official offered a poison pen to a Cuban for use against Castro while at the same time an emissary from President Kennedy was meeting with Castro to explore the possibility of improved relations."

Connolly on motorcades: Connally, testimony before the House Assassinations Committee, 1979.

Notes on Chapter Seven:
November 21, 1963

Congressman Gonzalez on Air Force One: Henry B. Gonzalez, interview with author.

Yarborough on Air Force One: Ralph Yarborough, interview with author; "long knives of Austin," is from Manchester, *Death of a President*, and Jerry Bruno diary, JFK Library.

Gonzalez on "how easy it would be": Gonzalez interview with author.

Arrival in Texas: John and Nellie Connally, testimony, WC, vol.4 and to House Assassinations Committee, 1979.

Scene at the Rice Hotel, Houston: Ralph Yarborough, interview with author; Connally, "Why Kennedy Came to Texas," *Life* magazine, November 22, 1967.

Connally's wild ride through Houston: Judge John V. Singleton, Jr., memoir attached to his oral history, LBJ Library, and interview with author.

Houston Chronicle poll: November 22, 1963; and Ralph Yarborough, interview with author.

Johnson and Kennedy at the Rice: Manchester, *Death of a President*, p. 82.

The distaste of many intelligent women for Connally: Liz Carpenter, interview with author.

Jackie Kennedy on Connally: her oral history, LBJ Library.

Notes on Chapter Eight:
November 22, 1963

JFK's medical therapies: Robert Dallek, *An Unfinished Life: John F. Kennedy, 1917-1963.*

JFK's fragile health: oral history, Dr. Janet Travell, interviewed by Theodore Sorenson, Dec. 26, 1974, John F. Kennedy Library, Boston.

JFK and amphetamine: In a *New York Times* article, December 4, 1972, it is suggested that JFK received amphetamine injections from Dr. Max Jacobson on two occasions: his first summit meeting with Nikita Khrushchev in Vienna, and before a 1961 speech on disarmament before the United Nations. Author interview with Lawrence Altman, M.D., a contributor to the article. See also *The Presidency of John F. Kennedy* by James Giglio.

Fatal corset: author's interview with Senator Ralph Yarborough.

Viewing the corset: author's examination of the corset with Dr. Lawrence Altman, M.D., National Archives, Feb. 11, 2013.

JFK quote on Connally-Yarborough rift and his premonition: Lawrence O'Brien, interview with author, and his book *No Final Victories*; and his testimony, WC, vol. 7

In the lobby of the Texas Hotel: Lawrence O'Brien, William Stinson, and Ralph Yarborough, interviews with author.

JFK to Connally at breakfast: Connally, *Life*, November 22, 1967; his testimony before House Assassinations Committee.

Connally's press conference in Texas Hotel: Kantor Exhibit 3, WC, vol.20; also Charles Roberts, oral history, JFK Library. In the Roberts oral history, he is asked if he thought the trip to Texas was succeeding in patching up the feuds in the Texas Democratic party. "We were not only under that impression, we had been told by some of the principals that [the trip] was having a therapeutic effect," Roberts replied. "Before leaving…Fort Worth, we had a quick session with Connally, and Connally gave us to understand that both the president and the vice president had pretty well impressed him [and Yarborough] with the necessity of closing ranks and burying the hatchet."

Kennedy-Johnson interchange in Fort Worth hotel: LBJ interview with Walter Cronkite, CBS, May 2, 1970.

The second premonition: Kenneth O'Donnell, testimony, WC, vol. 4; Manchester, *Death of a President*, p.121

Connally permission for Yarborough to sit at head table: Bishop, *Day Kennedy Was Shot*, p.124

The motorcade: William Stinson, Connally's aide in Dallas, drove the motorcade route with the author and provided recollections; Stinson also took the author to Parkland Hospital. For other recollections: Ralph Yarborough and Larry O'Brien, interviews with author; Charles Roberts, oral history, JFK Library.

Dialogue in presidential limousine: Connally, "Why Kennedy Came to Texas," *Life* magazine, November 22, 1967.

Sixth floor of the depository: Roy S. Truly testimony, WC, vols. 3 and 4.

Connally's flashback to his youth: Outtakes from interview conducted by Skip Hollandsworth, "USA Today on TV," February 20, 1989, provided to the author; Connally on "Geraldo" program, November 23, 1988; Manchester, *Death of a President*, p. 160

Nellie Connally's remark: her testimony before House Assassinations Committee, 1979.

On a normal physical reaction to a neck wound: Dr. Daniel Valaik, orthopedic surgeon, retired Navy seal, and head of orthopedics in Iraq for six years, interview with author, May 22, 2013.

Notes on Chapter Nine:
Parkland

Dialogue between Stinson and Dr. Red Duke: William Stinson, interview with author.

Connally's medical condition at Parkland: Dr. Charles Gregory and Dr. Robert Shaw, testimony, WC, vol. 4; William Stinson, interview with author; "Three Patients at Parkland," *Texas State Journal of Medicine*, vol. 60, January 1964.

Lyndon Johnson at Parkland: Henry Gonzalez, interview with author.

Dr. Charles James Carrico in Trauma Room #1: WC testimony, March 25, 1964.

Dr. Malcolm Oliver Perry on Kennedy's back brace: Assassination Records Review Board, August 1998.

Lady Bird's comfort for Jackie and Nellie: Lady Bird memo, June 15, 1964, special file on assassination, LBJ Library and her *White House Diary;* Manchester, *Death of a President,* p. 236.

LBJ drive to Love Field: Henry Wade, interview with author. Police officers joked with Wade later about LBJ's terror and undignified behavior.

Radio traffic from Air Force One: "Angel" recording, November 22, 1963, LBJ Library.

Lady Bird's actions: Liz Carpenter, recollections of November 22, 1963, manuscript, LBJ Library.

Notes on Chapter Ten:
The Conspiratorialists

"Not unhappy" and survivor's guilt: Interview on "60 Minutes," CBS February 28, 1988.

Horse meat and well-dressed goat: Dr. Alfred Oliver, testimony, WC, vol. 5.

Note on Reagan: John Pekkanan, an expert on the Reagan assassination attempt, interview with author.

Belin memo on Connally as target: Belin interview on "USA. Today on TV," February 20, 1988, and interview with author.

On Connally's bid to obtain the original Jan. 20, 1962 Oswald letter to him: Andy Kerr, *Journey among the Good and the Great.*

National Archives response: Marion Johnson, Warren Commission archivist, memo to the Archivist of the United States, October 12, 1967, and the archivist's negative response; Marion Johnson interview with the author.

Valenti and John P. Roche memos: Assassination File, LBJ Library; Jack Valenti, interview with author.

On "motor program": Dr. Thomas Gualtieri, an authority on neuropsychiatric disorders and their treatment. Dr. Richard Restak, interview, April 16, 2013.

Oswald was no jackal: From the Frederick Forsyth novel, *The Day of the Jackal*, based on the story of the actual professional assassin, Jean-Marie Bastien-Thiry, who was hired by elements of the French paramilitary group, OAS, to assassinate President Charles de Gaulle at Petit-Clamart on August 22, 1962.

On the best medical refutation of conspiracy theories, more than one shooter, more than three bullets: *Lincoln and Kennedy: Medical and Ballistic Comparisons of their Assassinations* by Dr. John K. Lattimer.